FISCHER'S CHOICE

A LIFE OF BRAM FISCHER

FISCHER'S CHOICE

A LIFE OF BRAM FISCHER

MARTIN MEREDITH

JONATHAN BALL PUBLISHERS
JOHANNESBURG & CAPE TOWN

ISBN 1 86842 131 7

Published in 2002 by
JONATHAN BALL PUBLISHERS (PTY) LTD
PO Box 33977
Jeppestown 2043

Design by Michael Barnett, Johannesburg
Reproduction of cover and picture sections by Collage Graphics, Johannesburg
Cover photograph by Eli Weinberg, by courtesy of *Sunday Times* Archives
Typesetting and reproduction of text by Alinea Studio, Cape Town
Printed and bound by CTP Book Printers, Caxton Street, Parow, Cape.

CONTENTS

I can no longer serve justice
in the way I have attempted to do
during the past thirty years.
I can only do it
in the way I have now chosen.

Bram Fischer

Bram Fischer could have become
prime minister or the chief justice of
South Africa if he had chosen to follow
the narrow path of Afrikaner nationalism.
He chose instead the long and
hard road to freedom
not only for himself but for all of us.

Nelson Mandela

ACKNOWLEDGEMENTS

On a spring day in 1997, I travelled to Bloemfontein in the old Orange Free State with Bram Fischer's daughters, Ruth and Ilse, to visit the past. We started at Hillandale, the farm just north of Bloemfontein where Bram's grandfather, Abraham Fischer, a former prime minister, had entertained in style and where Bram had spent several carefree years of his boyhood. Later, at the State Archives, we came across an exhibition of old photographs and newspaper cuttings outlining the events of Bram's life. We toured the elegant rooms of the Old Presidency, which British generals used as their headquarters during the Anglo-Boer War, and feasted on traditional Afrikaner dishes in the adjacent stables, now converted into a restaurant. We went next to Harmonie, the home where Bram married Molly Krige in a ceremony in a sunken area of the garden, under a pergola covered with wisteria, accompanied by songs sung by the household servants. Then we visited the *Vrouemonument*, an Afrikaner memorial to the deaths of thousands of women and children in British concentration camps during the Anglo-Boer War. And finally we went to the Garden of Remembrance where a simple plaque on a wall records Bram's passing; by government order, his ashes were retained by the Department of Prisons and have not been found. It was a day full of fond reminiscences, memorable in its own way.

There were many other memorable moments during the writing of this book. Nelson Mandela talked warmly about Bram in his home in Johannesburg, not far from the Fischers' Beaumont Street house which he often visited. Walter Sisulu recalled long discussions with Bram at Beaumont Street, where he sometimes stayed overnight. Many others were generous with their help. I am especially grateful to Beryl Baker, Esther Barsel, Mary Benson, Hilda Bernstein, Rusty Bernstein, George Bizos, John Bizzell, Mannie Brown, Pat Davidson, Denis Goldberg,

Miriam Hepner, Bob Hepple, Rica Hodgson, Joel Joffe, Adelaide Joseph, Paul Joseph, Kathy Kathrada, Hugh Lewin, John Loredo, Jean Middleton, Lesley Schermbrucker, Marius Schoon, Raymond Schoop, Mini Sepel, Ralph Sepel, Harold Strachan, Tim Wilson, AnnMarie Wolpe, and Harold Wolpe.

I have also benefited from access to the Fischer family archives, in particular to letters which Bram wrote to Molly, Ruth, Ilse and Paul. Reading them years later, they retain all the warmth, passion and consideration with which he wrote them. In prison, he used letters as a means of keeping himself involved in family life, thinking of presents and gifts for birthdays, advising on careers, musing about books and records as he would have done if he was free. They are part of the testimony of one of the most remarkable South Africans of the twentieth century.

PROLOGUE

In the early morning, as the security police kept watch on his house from the street outside, Bram Fischer wrote a farewell letter to his daughter Ilse.

'The sun is pouring into our garden, and presently I shall wake you up and we shall go out for what shall be one of our last swims. We shall look around at what has become a lovely place and both our hearts will be breaking because we shall know inevitably we had to leave it all.'

The revolutionary world that Bram Fischer inhabited was fast disintegrating. Almost all his group of fellow conspirators engaged in armed rebellion against the South African government had been arrested or had fled into exile. In his role as defence lawyer, Fischer had managed to save Nelson Mandela and other leading conspirators from the death penalty demanded by state prosecutors, but their sentence was nevertheless life imprisonment. Now Fischer himself was on trial for his involvement in the underground Communist Party which had helped organise the rebellion. What made the case especially grievous was that the chief witness against him was an old friend and colleague who had decided to betray him.

Though further resistance seemed hopeless, Fischer resolved to make one last defiant stand against the government. He was under no illusions about the difficulties or the risks. 'I have never had a more difficult decision to make – weighing the pros and cons was agony and I still don't know whether I am right,' he wrote. 'I think the main argument against my present plan remains that it might be a total flop, a James Bond that never got off the ground. In essence, this depends on how long I can keep it up. Real success will of course require me to carry on for a year or two but in fact I think that much less than that can be counted as "success".'

Later that morning, accompanied by Ilse, he made his way from the

1

kitchen through a connecting door to the garage and climbed into the back of a small Volkswagen, crouching low on the floor. Expecting the security police to pounce at any moment, Ilse drove out of the gate and took a circuitous route through the northern suburbs of Johannesburg to a block of flats in Killarney. Bram quickly got out of the car and moved away. Ilse had no idea of where he was going or when she would see him again.

Two days later, on Monday 25 January 1965, at the magistrate's court in central Johannesburg, the proceedings that Bram was due to attend opened as normal. Twelve defendants on trial with him filed into the courtroom to take their usual places; the prosecutors, the security police and the defence lawyers arrived in a group, talking in hushed tones; as the magistrate entered, all present stood.

Then Bram's counsel, Harold Hanson, rose to tell the court that he had received a letter from Accused Number One, explaining that he had decided to absent himself from the trial.

His sudden disappearance provoked astonishment. As a prominent lawyer who had once moved with ease in the highest political and social circles, he was a familiar public figure. Only recently he had returned to South Africa from a journey abroad, making clear his determination to face trial. To jump bail and abscond from court at this stage seemed inexplicable.

Inside the courtroom there was commotion. His fellow defendants seemed flabbergasted. The security police immediately launched a manhunt. As the hue and cry spread across South Africa, numerous sightings of him were reported. Some newspapers speculated that he had undergone plastic surgery; others claimed that he had been seen crossing the border into neighbouring Bechuanaland; or that he had reached Lusaka, the capital of Zambia.

'The desperate act of a desperate man,' proclaimed the prosecutor. 'The action of a coward.'

Yet Bram had set out his reasons with clear conviction in the letter read out to the court by Hanson that day. Bitterness and hatred of the government and its apartheid laws was mounting daily, he said. Unless the apartheid system was changed, the inevitable result would be bloodshed and civil war. 'What is needed is for white South Africans to shake themselves out of their complacency.'

It was especially important for Afrikaners like himself to stand against the government – indeed, it was 'a supreme duty' – because it was largely his 'fellow Afrikaners' who were responsible for the miseries and injustice of the apartheid system.

'If by my fight I can encourage even some people to think about, to understand and to abandon the policies they now so blindly follow, I shall not regret any punishment I may incur.'

He concluded: 'I can no longer serve justice in the way I have attempted to do during the past 30 years. I can do it only in the way I have now chosen.'

Bram was immensely proud of his Afrikaner heritage, but it made his task doubly difficult. As his friend Nelson Mandela observed in later years: 'He showed a level of courage and sacrifice that was in a class by itself. I fought only against injustice, not against my own people.'

CHAPTER ONE

BLOEMFONTEIN

Bram Fischer was born into one of the most distinguished Afrikaner families in the Orange Free State. The Fischers were part of the white elite in Bloemfontein, a small but increasingly prosperous town lying on the great plains north of the Orange River, which served as the capital for the young Afrikaner republic during the nineteenth century. Bram's grandfather, Abraham Fischer, had arrived there in 1875, a newly qualified lawyer moving north from the Cape Town area where the Fischers had settled in the eighteenth century. His young wife, Ada Robertson, was the daughter of Scottish immigrants whom he had married two years before.

The Fischers soon established a prominent role in political and social life. They acquired an imposing double-storey mansion, Fern Lodge, with spacious gardens running down to the Bloemfontein Spruit, and a farm a few miles north of the town which they called Hillandale. Bram was elected to the Volksraad, the Orange Free State parliament, where he was much valued for his wise counsel. They entertained in a grand manner both in their townhouse and at their farm. Every year they gave a huge banquet for members of the Volksraad. They were renowned too for their play productions: Abraham painted the stage scenery and directed the plays.

Their farm, Hillandale, was a place of special importance to them. The house they built there stood on a rocky *kopje* overlooking the plains. Abraham Fischer delighted in planting trees, particularly willows and karees, in tending his orchards and taking long, rambling walks through the bush. At Christmas time, the Fischers would give a lunch for a score of guests, setting out tables under the almond trees. Tennis and croquet parties were a regular event. At the Fischers' silver wedding anniversary in October 1898, 100 guests came to Hillandale to celebrate, among them President Martinus Steyn and his wife.

Bloemfontein too flourished during these years. The first railway from the Cape Colony opened in 1890. A new parliament building – the Raadzaal – was inaugurated in 1893, sufficiently grand for what was termed a 'model Republic'. During the 1890s, new schools, a hospital, a post office building and a club were constructed. While Bloemfontein remained essentially a small town, with a white population numbering only about 2 500, it possessed a cosmopolitan atmosphere, with its own orchestra, church and choral societies, language study circles, Shakespeare readings, dances and amateur theatricals, parks and public gardens. Visitors from Europe were given a warm welcome. Although only Dutch was permitted in the Volksraad, English was commonly spoken in town and business life. The writer Anthony Trollope once described Bloemfontein as the most 'English' town he had visited in southern Africa.

All this, however, was overshadowed by the growing threat of war. The discovery of gold in 1886 had turned the neighbouring Afrikaner republic of the Transvaal into the richest state in southern Africa and made Britain, then at the peak of its imperial fortunes, ambitious to gain control. An attempted *coup d'état* in 1895, engineered by mining magnates with the connivance of British ministers, failed ignominiously, but Britain nevertheless remained intent on extending the realms of its empire.

As the threat of war drew closer, Abraham Fischer, with his long white beard and glass eye that he had worn since a boyhood accident, became an increasingly central figure in the drama. Appointed by President Steyn to the executive council of the Orange Free State in 1896, he was constantly on the move, endeavouring to work out a negotiated settlement between the two sides. In Pretoria, President Kruger urged him to join the Transvaal government as state secretary, but Fischer was wary of the 'queer folk' who surrounded Kruger and the corruption rife in his regime, and declined to take on the job. He was equally distrustful of the British high commissioner, Lord Milner, who seemed to him to be bent on war whatever the cost.

When Kruger and Milner met for the first time at the presidency in Bloemfontein in May 1899, Fischer was present as one of the principal negotiators. To ensure that they were comfortably accommodated, Gustav Fichardt, a wealthy businessman, offered Milner his house,

Kayalami, as a residence, while his son, Charlie Fichardt, made his double-storeyed house in Elizabeth Street available to Kruger. But despite the pleasantries, nothing was accomplished. For several months longer, Fischer and Steyn strove to avoid conflict, but to no avail.

As he was driving in his carriage across Market Square in Bloemfontein, the capital of the Orange Free State, shortly before war broke out, Fischer stopped briefly to tell Gustav Fichardt how negotiations were progressing. 'We have given the last concession we possibly can,' he said. 'If war comes now, even I, who have worked so hard for peace, would feel justified in going out to fight – if with my one eye I would be of any use.'

Even though the risks of defeat were high, when members of the Free State Volksraad met in secret to decide whether to stand together with their fellow Afrikaners in the Transvaal to defy the might of the British army, their view was unanimous, as Fischer recorded. 'There was no bounce or *grootpraat* [boasting] but quiet determination, and the spontaneous and unmistakable enthusiasm with which the members burst out into the Volkslied [the national anthem] was something to remember. They were all most cheerful learning that the best had been done to avert war and that they were unjustly being dragged into it.'

The Fischer family was scattered by the tide of war. In March 1900, Abraham Fischer, accompanied by his wife, Ada, sailed from Portuguese East Africa for Europe as part of an official delegation seeking support for the Boer cause from European governments, and they were unable to return home until after the war had ended. Their elder son, Harry, who was then 25 years old, served in Boer commandos in the Orange Free State, before being taken prisoner. Their younger son, Percy, Bram's father, who was then 21 years old, was meanwhile studying law at Cambridge University, a student in enemy territory constantly fretting at missing the action with his compatriots.

Bloemfontein meanwhile became an occupied town under the control of a large British garrison. By British edict, the Orange Free State was renamed the Orange River Colony. The Fischers' townhouse, Fern Lodge, was commandeered by the British authorities. Their English governess, Nakie Smith, who had remained behind, later described how British soldiers occupying the house had torn up editions of Dickens to stuff their pillows with the pages. Their farm, Hillandale, was turned into a British supply depot.

The war brought devastation to the Orange Free State and the Transvaal on an appalling scale. Faced with guerrilla warfare for which they were ill-prepared, British military commanders resorted to a scorched earth strategy in which Boer villages were razed to the ground, thousands of Boer farmsteads destroyed, and cattle and sheep slaughtered or carried away in such numbers that by the end of the war the Boers of the Orange Free State had lost half of their herds, and those in the Transvaal three-quarters. In a despatch to London in 1901, Lord Milner described the Orange Free State as 'virtually a desert'.

Women and children were rounded up and placed in what the British called concentration camps. The site of the Bloemfontein camp was at Spitskop, a hillside two miles from the town where hundreds of women and children were dumped in tents on a barren stretch of *veldt* without any trees or shade. Conditions in the concentration camps, like the one at Spitskop, were so primitive that some 26 000 Boers died there from disease and malnutrition, most of them children under the age of 16.

The aftermath of the war was made even more bitter by Milner's determined efforts to anglicise the Boer population. At Milner's insistence, English was made the official language, even though Boers outnumbered British. In the Orange River Colony and the Transvaal the whole education system was swept away and replaced by an English-dominated one. But rather than submit to Milner's schemes, Afrikaner leaders founded their own private schools which used Dutch as well as English as a medium of instruction, and promoted a sense of Afrikaner national consciousness among students. By the time Milner left South Africa in 1905, all that he had achieved was a depth of hostility among Afrikaners greater than anything that had existed before the war, and the stirrings of a new Afrikaner nationalism.

A change of government in Britain later that year led to a more enlightened policy. By 1906, only four years after a devastating war of conquest, Britain agreed to hand back the Orange River Colony and the Transvaal as self-governing territories. And in November

1907, after a general election, a new government in Bloemfontein was sworn in. Its prime minister was Abraham Fischer.

Percy Fischer, meanwhile, had returned from Cambridge to embark on his own career as a lawyer. As well as establishing a law practice, he lectured at the local college. In April 1907 he married Ella Fichardt, the younger daughter of Gustav Fichardt, whom he had known since childhood. The marriage linked two of the most prominent families in Bloemfontein. An immigrant from Germany, Gustav Fichardt had developed his supply store into the most prestigious and profitable business in Bloemfontein. At the outbreak of war, the firm of GA Fichardt had been appointed as commissariat of the Free State army.

Bram Fischer was born a year later, on 23 April 1908. The name by which he was baptised was Abram, an Afrikaans contraction of his grandfather's name, Abraham, but from the start his parents called him Bram, pronouncing it as 'Braam'. His childhood, though happy and secure, was marked by the turbulence of the times. For the fierce emotions stirred up by the Anglo-Boer War and its cruel aftermath still reverberated across the country.

Abraham Fischer's task as prime minister was to deal with Boer grievances and hardships resulting from the war whilst at the same time accommodating the realities of British hegemony. As part of their grand scheme for southern Africa, the British devised plans for a union between the two former Boer republics of the Orange Free State and the Transvaal, and the two British colonies of the Cape and Natal. The hope was that the Boers and the British might find a way of resolving their differences and merge into a single South African nation. Fischer attended several conferences preparing the way for union, and travelled to London with Ada in 1909 for further negotiations. At a Buckingham Palace function, Ada was seated next to Lord Milner, but managed to make clear her disdain for him. 'I almost pitied the man,' Abraham wrote to Percy, 'he seemed so out of it.'

When the Union of South Africa was launched in 1910, Abraham Fischer, along with other prominent Afrikaner leaders, accepted a position in the Union government. Outwardly there seemed a reasonable prospect that reconciliation might work. Yet fear and resentment of British domination ran deep. Many Afrikaners never accepted the idea of being part of the British Empire, and mourned the loss of their own republics. Everywhere they were reminded of the presence of British authority. *God Save The King* became the official anthem. The national flag was a British Red Ensign, with the Union Coat of Arms in a lower corner. The British dominated industry, commerce and the mines, and controlled banks and finance houses. Moreover, under the 1910 constitution, on questions of war and peace South Africa was not a sovereign independent state but was bound by decisions of the British government.

Fearing that the sheer weight of British influence would engulf the Afrikaner people and turn South Africa into a mere appendage of the British Empire, a group of prominent Afrikaners began openly to repudiate the government's policy of reconciliation. Foremost among them was one of Abraham Fischer's closest colleagues, General Barry Hertzog, a former Free State commando leader who had served in Fischer's government in the Orange River Colony before accepting an appointment as minister in the Union government in 1910.

When Hertzog was forced out of the Union government in 1912, Fischer was left in a quandary as to whether to follow him or support the government. By choosing to remain in the government, he earned himself the censure of his supporters in the Orange Free State. A formal vote of no confidence there left him dispirited and disheartened, and in ailing health he began to withdraw from political activity. When he died on 16 November 1913, at the age of 63, all the public buildings in Bloemfontein were closed as a mark of respect.

The outbreak of war between Britain and Germany in 1914 brought about a deep rift in the Afrikaner community. Faced with a British request for South African forces to invade German South West Africa (Namibia), General Louis Botha felt obliged to accede. But many Afrikaners were outraged that South Africa should be drawn into the conflict on Britain's side. 'This is a war between England and Germany,' declared Hertzog. 'It is not a South African war.' Several of his old Boer War colleagues thought the time was ripe for rebellion, and issued a call to arms.

Once again, the fortunes of the Fischer family were blighted by war. Rumours were rife that the Afrikaner rebels were acting in league with Germany. Afrikaner politicians like Hertzog were accused of being 'German agents'. As rebel forces gained control of great

10

swathes of the Free State and the western Transvaal, a mood of jingoism swept through many South African towns, fanned by extremist groups like the British Citizens Movement. Shops and businesses with German names became the target for attack. At the age of six, sitting on his father's shoulders, Bram Fischer watched as mobs in Bloemfontein set fire to business premises with German names, including those of his mother's family, the Fichardts.

Bram's parents remained resolutely sympathetic to the rebels. When sporadic clashes between government troops and rebel forces broke out in the Free State, Ella wrote to the local Bloemfontein newspaper, *The Friend*, appealing for medical assistance for wounded personnel. Within a few hours of its publication, an old lady walked across the town to deliver a mosquito net. The Fischers' house in Reitz Street – 'Harmonie' – was soon inundated with offers of help, as Ella recorded in an account written many years later. 'Doctors drew up lists of ambulance requirements; carpenters came forward with offers to provide the material and make the splints; farmers offered the necessary trolley wagons, horses and saddles; school teachers gave liberally of their savings; students haunted the houses where preparations were being made; women from all stations of life sewed hospital shirts, padded splints and cotton wool bandages, and made red cross flags and arm bandages.' Wounded rebels arriving at the old National Hospital in Bloemfontein were provided with Bibles, books and cigarettes.

Much of the work was carried out surreptitiously. 'No books could be kept, no list of subscribers, no minutes of meetings. In fact generous donors asked that there should be no records kept of their gifts, no receipts given. For the slightest evidence might turn the scales against a law-abiding and upright citizen. Would-be helpers had to come after dark by devious ways – sometimes over backyard fences and in at kitchen doors, to centres where their help was needed.'

Percy Fischer helped organise an ambulance unit and, with government permission, set off on horseback with other volunteers in search of rebel commandos. But after three months of sporadic encounters, the rebellion collapsed.

In Bloemfontein, Percy worked tirelessly in the courts defending rebels whom the government brought to trial, while Ella joined a group of prison visitors taking rebel prisoners food and flowers, sometimes allowing Bram to accompany her. Bram retained vivid memories of those visits to prison. One of his most treasured possessions was a wood carving of a chameleon with moving parts, made especially for him by the *kommandant* of the Kroonstad commando while awaiting trial.

In a conciliatory gesture, the government decided to deal leniently with the rebels. Most were given no more than fines. General Christiaan de Wet, the Free State rebel leader, was sentenced to six years' imprisonment but served only two.

But Percy Fischer's actions in defending the rebels cost him dearly. Clients shunned him, and attorneys declined to send him briefs. So difficult did his circumstances become that he was obliged to rent out his house in Reitz Street and move his growing family – four children and a pregnant wife – to a small shack on a section of the Hillandale farm, known as Bergendal, which he had inherited from Abraham. To make ends meet, Ella was reduced to selling flowers at Bloemfontein station.

For young Bram, seven years old at the time, Bergendal offered endless possibilities of excitement and adventure. He came to know every inch of its terrain, every aspect of life in the bush, spending hours on horseback and on long walks, exploring river beds, swimming and boating in dams, absorbed by the trees and the wildlife around him. His father, Percy, was a knowledgeable guide, passing on the folklore of the bush he had learned during his own boyhood on Hillandale. Sunday expeditions across the *veldt* were undertaken as enthusiastically as they had been during Abraham Fischer's day.

The Fischer household was notable for its open-minded outlook. Around the dinner table, conversation was lively and argumentative, conducted in both English and Afrikaans. The Fischer children – four boys and a girl – were all encouraged to develop inquiring minds and wide interests. Their father was apt to engage any passing child in discussion.

At school, Bram showed promise as both scholar and sportsman. Though short in stature, like both his parents, and slightly built, he possessed abundant willpower. At Grey College in Bloemfontein, a school which took both English and Afrikaans-speaking pupils, he was chosen as editor of the school journal. During his final year there, he became junior tennis champion of the Free State. He also played for the school's first team in rugby and cricket. His teachers admired both his talents and his modest and unassuming nature.

One teacher in particular had a profound impact on him. Leo Marquard, a young history master, recently returned from Oxford, inspired students by his energetic nature and liberal approach. He often invited students to afternoon tea to meet overseas visitors, and took them on camping trips for study and debate. A former Rhodes scholar, from a distinguished Afrikaner family, he founded the National Union of South African Students (Nusas), serving as its president for seven years. With his wife, Nell, he formed the centre of what for Bram was to become a 'magic circle'.

The Fischer family fortunes had meanwhile recovered. Once the animosities of the 1914 rebellion had abated, Percy Fischer managed to re-establish his law practice and gained increasing prominence as a lawyer. The family moved back to Harmonie in Reitz Street, enlarging it with a swimming pool and a tennis court. Once again they were part of the Bloemfontein elite.

In 1926, at the age of 17, Bram went to Cape Town University to study economics and history. He immersed himself in Cape Town life, enjoying a lively social round of dances, concerts, picnics, hikes, swimming and tennis parties. As a member of an eminent Afrikaner family, he was welcomed by the political establishment. He was invited by the Hertzogs to spend a weekend at the prime minister's residence at Groote Schuur. He paid several visits to Ouma Steyn, the widow of the last president of the Orange Free State. He listened to debates in parliament and kept abreast of political gossip.

Despite the attractions of Cape Town, Bram had wider ambitions and set his sights on winning a Rhodes scholarship to Oxford. Because competition for the award was less stiff in the Orange Free State than in the Cape Province, he decided to transfer to Grey University College in Bloemfontein. Thus in 1927 Bram returned home to Harmonie and re-entered the 'magic circle' of Leo and Nell Marquard.

Among his other activities, Leo Marquard was increasingly involved in trying to build bridges between the races of South Africa.

13

In 1927 he helped to launch the Bloemfontein branch of the Joint Council of Europeans and Africans, a national organisation intended to provide a forum where whites and blacks, mainly teachers and clergymen, could meet to discuss African conditions. Bram was asked to join.

At his first meeting, an incident occurred which he was to remember vividly for the rest of his life. As Marquard introduced him to leading members of the African community, Bram felt a sudden revulsion at having to shake their hands. The enormous effort of will it took he was never to forget.

That night he spent hours trying to account for his reaction. During his childhood at Bergendal, he had spent countless days in the company of two African youths of his own age, roaming the farm, hunting, modelling clay oxen, playing and swimming together, and not once during those years could he remember that 'the colour of our skins affected our fun or our quarrels or our close friendship in any way'.

Then, when his family had moved back to town, he had drifted into the habit common to most white South Africans of regarding whites as masters and Africans simply as servants. Now he seemed unable to take the hand of a black man in friendship. 'What became abundantly clear was that it was I and not the black man who had changed,' he recalled. 'I had developed an antagonism for which I could find no rational basis whatsoever.'

Later that year, Bram became involved in adult education courses for Africans in Waaihoek 'location' in Bloemfontein, where he taught reading and writing in a dilapidated building with winter winds blowing dust through the makeshift classroom. And there he began to realise that real friendship could extend across the colour bar.

Yet in other respects Bram remained a conventional young Afrikaner nationalist. He was firmly convinced that the government's policy of segregation offered the only solution to South Africa's racial problems. Like his parents, he harboured an abiding hatred of the British Empire and all that it stood for. At school he vowed never to wear a cadet force uniform because of its association with British rule. When the Prince of Wales passed through Bloemfontein during a tour of South Africa in 1925, Bram joined other students in refusing to welcome him. During the election in 1924 he cheered loudly every time a success for General Hertzog's National Party was announced.

The climax to his enthusiasm for the National Party came in 1929 when he stood as a National Party candidate for election to the post of prime minister in a student 'parliament' held under the auspices of the National Union of South African Students (Nusas). Leo Marquard had hoped that Bram might be persuaded to step out of the mould of South African politics, but Bram preferred to follow a more 'patriotic' line. He argued in favour of abolishing the British veto over South African legislation, and ending the jurisdiction of the Privy Council in London as the final arbiter in the administration of justice. After a vigorous campaign, he won the election.

When Bram turned 21 in 1929, shortly after graduating with distinction from Grey University College, his parents arranged a formal dinner and dance for him at Harmonie, inviting 100 guests. To many present, Bram seemed on the brink of a brilliant career, a favoured son of Afrikanerdom, well-connected and widely admired for his many talents. To mark the occasion, Ouma Steyn, the *grande dame* of the old Orange Free State, sent a message of congratulations: 'As a child and as a student you have set an example to all. I know that Bram Fischer is going to play an honourable role in the history of South Africa.'

CHAPTER 2

LOVE AND COMMUNISM

Like his father and his grandfather before him, Bram decided on a
career as a lawyer. In 1929 he started work as registrar in the Supreme
Court of the Orange Free State, while studying part-time for a law
degree at Grey University College. His work included travelling on
circuit court to different towns in the Orange Free State, accompanying
the judge-president, Sir Etienne de Villiers, on his rounds.

He pursued a wide range of other activities, editing the Nusas
journal and revelling in competitive sport. In 1928 he was selected to
play as scrum half for the Free State rugby team in a match against
the All Blacks of New Zealand. As well as teaching literacy classes in
Waaihoek location, he gathered evidence for the Joint Council on
conditions in African employment, housing, health and welfare to
present to the Native Economic Commission. In his testimony before
a hearing of the commission in Bloemfontein, he argued against
segregation and in favour of the free flow of labour from the African
reserves to the towns. In 1930 he learnt that his application for a
Rhodes scholarship had been approved.

But what transformed his life most of all was an encounter with a
high-spirited girl with blue eyes, brown curls and a wild streak. He
had first met Molly Krige at the Ramblers Club in Bloemfontein in
1927; Molly went there as a member of the women's hockey team
from Transvaal University College. Three years later, while travelling
as registrar on circuit court with Sir Etienne de Villiers, Bram met her
again in Bethlehem, a town in the eastern Free State where Molly had
taken a post as a teacher. From then on, Bram made every excuse to
return to Bethlehem.

Molly came from an Afrikaner family with a lineage as distinguished as that of the Fischers. Her father, 'Tottie' Krige, had served
during the First World War as an aide-de-camp to General Jan Smuts,

16

then minister of defence and a member of the British war cabinet; her aunt, Issie, was married to Smuts, who, after the war, remained one of South Africa's most prominent politicians. Her mother, Emelie Bernsmann, was the daughter of a German missionary who had been stationed in South West Africa. Though well-connected, the Kriges were not wealthy. 'Tottie' Krige worked as a land surveyor and brought up his family on a smallholding in Silverton, near Pretoria. Molly attended an English school, Pretoria Girls' High, but at home spoke Afrikaans. Her ambition had been to train as a veterinarian, but because the family was short of funds, she became a teacher instead.

Her first post was at Housecroft School in Bethlehem, where her spirited nature won her popularity among pupils but caused some disquiet among the school's managers. She loved going on midnight walks and midnight swims, getting wet in the rain and walking barefoot through mud. And, at night, she enjoyed secretly visiting the Bethlehem cemetery.

It was there, on a moonlit summer's night in January 1931, that Bram finally broke through her reluctance to surrender her independence. 'I suppose I might as well leap,' she said to him.

In a passionate letter from the Grand Hotel in Ladybrand the following day, Bram wrote:

I love you. I love you. I love you. This sounds like the beginning of a Court Circular. I wish I could make it the beginning of many happy years for you. But I've been terribly afraid today. Falling in love is a funny thing. At first you spend most of the time wondering whether you've really fallen in love. That seems to be the only really exciting time. After that it hurts so much that you often wish it had not happened at all. That is when you fancy that once you've heard what you told me last night, all your troubles will disappear.

But the opposite was also possible.

Now I'm feeling terrible. Were you sure of what you said? And even if you were, haven't I taken on too big a thing? But if it

17

wasn't just the moon and the cemetery, please write and tell me – just once more – that you love me.

Another passionate letter followed, a week later:

> I adore you Molly, simply all the time. I dream about you for at least 90 per cent of the day, and don't escape even at night. Whatever you care to call it, it's the first thing in eight years that I've believed in absolutely and without question. I have reasoned about it too and it has supplied an essential to my credo that has been missing thus far and that I'll never lose, no matter what happens. It's wonderful to have found something you can believe in in this world ... You have let me kiss you – and that will remain the greatest thing in my life until – perhaps – one day, you kiss me – a mad dream.

Molly's replies were more hesitant. She told Bram she did not want him to take her seriously or to get to know her well.

> I don't know how to start the serious stuff I promised you. You see I know quite well what I'm responsible for. I've made several people unhappy and incapable of enjoying simple pleasures like the sun and the wind and the rain. It's simply because I fall in and out of love very easily – and never worry if I hurt people because I'm much too frivolous to get hurt myself. The only times when I'm really unhappy is when I can't decide with whom I ought to fall in love – or how to tell someone that I've changed my mind.

As the journey between Bloemfontein and Bethlehem involved a five-hour car ride, they sometimes could not meet from one week to the next, and kept in touch through frequent letters. At Easter in 1933 they spent an exhilarating weekend together, riding and swimming, on a friend's farm at Lusthof in the eastern Free State, with spectacular views of the Maluti mountains on the horizon. But still Molly kept her distance. When Bram encouraged her to visit Harmonie to meet his parents, she seemed reluctant, telling Bram she did not want to 'worry' his family. To Bram's exasperation, her letters were often brief

18

and evasive, giving little away about herself. She claimed that the reason she never wrote 'serious' letters, which Bram constantly urged her to do, was because she could not believe that anyone would have the slightest interest in anything she had to say.

While Bram viewed the idea of marriage warmly, Molly made it clear she was in no hurry. When Bram fretted that because of the great depression of the early 1930s it might be years before he could earn enough to marry, she replied:

> I wish you wouldn't be so foolish. Do you really think that a couple of years either way is going to make any difference to me as long as I'm in love with you? If I ever 'leap back' that won't have anything to do with it and even if I do change my mind – or you do – I'll never regret this glorious 'game' – and besides – I'm quite serious now – I don't want to get married for the next 10 or 12 years – not even to you. So for heaven's sake ... please don't reproach yourself for anything while I'm perfectly happy.

Bram's winning of a Rhodes scholarship to Oxford anyway meant that they would be separated for several years. He viewed the prospect with some misgivings, admitting to Molly that he had never done anything for which he felt less inclined. On the night before his departure by train from Bloemfontein, he and his mother wandered about the house drinking whisky and shedding tears. Before setting sail from Cape Town on 18 December 1931, he wrote to Molly:

> Goodbye, Molly ... You've given me the two most wonderful years I've ever had ... Will you write and tell me whenever you cry? And by the way, I still love you for ever – just in case I haven't told you before.

Bram's arrival in Oxford on a winter's afternoon in January 1932 was hardly auspicious. 'It was bleak and cold and when I drove up to New College between high walls black with age, I felt just as if I were going to prison,' he wrote to Molly. Within a week he injured his knee in a rugby match and spent four weeks in hospital. His walk was never the same again.

19

Bram found it difficult to acclimatise. 'Here,' he wrote to Molly, 'there's never any rain and there's never any sun and I know at Lusthof there are blue skies and every afternoon huge thunderclouds, so let's go and lie in the grass near Salpeterkrans and watch the *krantz* [cliff] slowly toppling over us as the clouds shift over Basutoland.'

But Oxford soon opened him to new influences. It was a time of ideological ferment, of mass unemployment, hunger marches and financial crises, of fierce dissension over the merits of capitalism and communism. Oxford offered a choice between the October Club which celebrated the Russian revolution, Oswald Mosley's Fascist Club, or the Labour Club, brimful of socialists. Bram gravitated towards the Labour Club – 'quite the most wideawake political club in Oxford', he wrote. He was present when the Oxford Union carried by a substantial majority the resolution that 'this House will not fight for King and Country'.

He also began to take an interest in the Soviet Union. 'I always have a sort of feeling that I should go and see Russia,' he wrote to Molly. Along with three Oxford friends, in the summer of 1932, he prepared to travel to the Soviet Union, reading biographies of Lenin and studies of Stalin's Five Year Plan. 'My head's crammed with statistics, foreign names and political constitutions,' he wrote. Through the state agency, Intourist, he and his friends arranged a three-week journey across Russia, covering some 6 000 miles by train and by boat.

They set sail for Leningrad from Hay's Wharf near London Bridge on 25 June in a 3 000-ton Soviet ship named *Ruszutak*. On board were Russian families working in London returning home on holiday, Americans going to work in the Soviet Union, and a small number of tourists. Bram noted that the tourists were 'more extremely communistic than the Russians themselves'.

In Leningrad they embarked on a hectic round of visits to museums, opera houses and sports institutions. In Moscow they visited Red Square and gazed at Lenin's tomb illuminated at night. Before leaving for Nizhni Novgorod (Gorki), Bram wrote to Molly from the New Moscow Hotel: 'If you have stopped loving me by the time I get back to Leningrad on the 18th, I'll just stay here and become a Bolshevik!'

From Nizhni Novgorod they travelled by riverboat some 1 700 miles along the Volga to Stalingrad, then on to Rostov on the Black

Sea, by train through the Ukraine to Kiev, then back to Leningrad. Along the way, they visited a state farm and workers' clubs.

In letters home, Bram gave his impressions from this whirlwind tour. He spoke of the advances the Soviet Union had made in establishing heavy industry by eliminating the opportunity for private profit, but questioned whether the same degree of incentive could be provided under communism as under capitalism. He admired its artistic achievements, describing how some 50 theatres and operas were open in Moscow every evening, and how film and theatre directors were experimenting with new techniques; but he also referred to the ruthless control exercised by the secret police. He was particularly impressed by the way, he said, that the Soviet Union, with more than a hundred nationalities, had found a solution to the nationalities problem, comparing it favourably to the difficulties experienced in South Africa between the English and the Afrikaners. 'It is wonderful how the Bolsheviks have overcome all the problems that we have in South Africa, where there are only two nations,' he wrote, forgetting to mention the Africans.

For the rest of the summer of 1932, Bram roamed around Europe, enjoying its art galleries and its architecture, delving into some more avant-garde corners and endlessly discussing politics. In the Latvian capital, Riga, he attended an international student conference, then travelled on to Berlin, Dresden, Prague, Vienna and Salzburg.

On the journey back from Salzburg, Bram had an amorous encounter about which he felt obliged to tell Molly. 'A very charming young German girl from the university of Berlin wanted me to stay on with her at München where we could register as husband and wife.' He had resisted the temptation, he wrote, but added, 'just why is difficult to say'. The event prompted him to question whether it was possible to have a number of sexual relationships but still love only one person. In his view, sex and love were not identical, and physical fidelity was not an absolute good. He was sure that he could love Molly even if she had lived with other men. But he confessed this to her in trepidation, fearing that she might now want to end their relationship.

Molly replied that she was not shocked since she already knew his wider views on morality. 'That was one of the reasons I loved you best – I mean that you didn't look for evil where there was none.' But she questioned Bram's assertion that he would not mind if she had in fact lived with other men. 'I do think that you would mind very much and that you would have been far less tolerant yourself, if you had actually tried out your own philosophy. You're rather a dear you know. You have such "frightfully loose moral standards" and then you never do a thing to be ashamed of.'

For the summer of 1933, Bram returned to Europe but, with Hitler's rise to power in Germany, the mood was more ominous. An international student conference he attended in Bavaria was overshadowed by the growing menace of Nazism and its threat to the Jewish population – 'Five days ago the law was finalised permitting the forced sterilisation of any unwanted element (the Jews),' he wrote. He described some German students he met as charming and 'frightfully sincere'. In Vienna, he made a point of looking up old 'Nazi friends'. But, he told his father in a letter home, he regarded Nazism as a 'cancerous nationalism' – 'The whole movement is hateful – but the difficulty is that the Germans will probably make a success of it.'

Staying at the Hotel Seeblick in Grundlsee in the Austrian alps, he found the place 'crammed with Socialists and Jews'. The talk was all of underground resistance, bombs and revolutionary cells. 'The communists in Germany are talking about the revolution there within six months or a year, but according to the best opinion, they are talking through their hats. There seems to be a notion that the very shortest possible life of the Hitler regime will be ten years.'

Bram developed from these experiences a profound antipathy to nationalism. 'I believe firmly that the world's one hope of salvation lies in the suppression of ... nationalism,' he wrote to his father, 'and if a person takes that point of view, it's difficult to generate much enthusiasm for the birth ... of exactly that spirit in our country.' What was needed instead was to become internationalist in outlook, and strive for the actual scientific organisation of the whole world.

Bram dwelt on the same theme later in the year at a dinner at the Restaurant Frascati in London. It was held to commemorate Dingaan's Day, the anniversary of the Battle of Blood River in 1836 when a small party of Voortrekkers defeated the might of the Zulu army, usually an occasion for much celebration among Afrikaner nationalists. The printed programme was emblazoned with an

Afrikaans poem entitled *Afrikaner Landgenote* [Afrikaner Country-men], urging Afrikaners to *'wees getrou aan volk en taal'* [be true to *volk* and language]. In notes he prepared for his speech, Bram warned of the dangers implicit in the rise of German nationalism; the threat to peace could not be overestimated. Then he added, 'It behoves us to examine our own youthful nationalism with great care.'

> Time out of number we have heard Blood River referred to as bringing the boon of European civilisation to southern Africa. But one point of view I have never heard Dingaan's Day considered from is the point of view of Dingaan ... The time has come, if it is not already growing late, for an acute examination of this attitude ... I would not attempt to minimise the tasks. Many ideas as to race and nationality have to be destroyed or modified. This will require a new attitude of mind – of all human qualities perhaps the most difficult to attain ... In September 1935 it will be a hundred years since Van Rensburg and Trichardt crossed the Orange River ... Now another great effort is needed, but it must be integrating this time, and draw together not only the two different European races, but see to it that these two advance with our vast black population.

Bram's three years in Oxford soon passed. In 1933 he was elected president of the prestigious Ralegh Club whose members were drawn from all parts of the British Empire. He obtained a degree in jurisprudence and a diploma in economics. When the time came for him to leave in the summer of 1934, the secretary of the Rhodes Trust, CK Allen, wrote a report describing him as 'one of the most delightful of the Rhodes scholars from any country, and a man who has won universal esteem and affection'.

Rather than settle for the comforts of Bloemfontein, Bram decided to launch his career as an advocate in Johannesburg, the mining and industrial centre of South Africa where the opportunities were greater. Another advantage was that it was closer to Pretoria where Molly was now working. He established chambers with other young advocates and turned his hand to everything from divorce to murder. In court he gained a reputation for being methodical, conscientious and invariably well prepared. He also began to take an interest in mining law, and soon developed an expertise that mining companies valued. His career as a successful lawyer seemed assured.

Molly, however, he found difficult to pin down. In his absence she had formed an attachment to a talented young politician, Jan Hofmeyr, and though she saw little future in it she was reluctant to break off the relationship altogether. In 1934 her mother died, leaving Molly prone to fits of depression and anxiety. Towards Bram she remained affectionate. They went to dances and plays and took up a new pleasure – golf. In December 1935 they spent an idyllic week together during a holiday the Fischer family organised at Umtentweni on the Natal coast, going for midnight swims, walking through the forests, taking trips by car. Bram was enraptured by it all. Afterwards he wrote:

> The funny part about it now is that I don't know whether I want to cry for loneliness or because I'm terribly happy. Things seem to have become so much more real during the last week. I can see many pictures of you – pictures of Lusthof, pictures at Silverton or Bethlehem. I used to think they were vivid, but now they seem to be pale and distant. Now when I think of you in the forest – your body speckled with sun and shade or pale under the grey clouds – or when I think of your eyes suddenly green and your soft hair against a sand dune, my pictures are warm and living. I can feel you as I said goodbye to you in the train. I can even put my head on your breasts. Oh sweetheart, please believe what I told you that there is nothing but you in the world for me – nothing, nothing is worthwhile unless I can share it with you.

Molly, too, thought that the week at Umtentweni had been the most wonderful experience of her life. But, she told Bram, she would stay no longer than a week because she always felt the need to be free to leave places when she wanted.

In April 1936 Molly left Pretoria to take up a post as a teacher for one year in Windhoek, the capital of South West Africa, 1 000 miles away. Her reason for leaving, she explained to Bram, had nothing to do with him:

It's not because I doubt your feelings towards me and it's not because I'm not sure that I love you – because I am and I know I'm going to marry you and be happy ever after no matter what you say about it – but darling, I'm so dreadfully unsure of myself in my dealings with myself ... I know that sounds dreadful, but it's true. I have never yet found out who I am or what I am.

Though initially horrified by Molly's decision to go, Bram came to accept her need for independence. Her stay in Windhoek, he suggested, would be good for both of them. Molly too began to change her mind. Soon after arriving in Windhoek, she wrote to say she would marry him at any time. In June 1936 they planned to become formally engaged during a school vacation. Molly gave Bram strict instructions: 'You're not to ask my father to marry me – I won't be bargained over. I mean if I say I'll marry you, we don't have to ask anyone else, we'll just tell them and there you are. I'll probably mention it to him quite casually myself.'

However, there were further delays. At the end of her year's contract in Windhoek, Molly took the opportunity to travel to Europe. Bram encouraged her, helping with the preparations and providing lists of contacts, hoping her experiences would be as enthralling as his had been. It was not until August 1937 that Molly returned to South Africa.

The wedding finally took place on 18 September that year at Harmonie in Bloemfontein. In a sunken area of the garden, under a pergola covered with wisteria, Molly and Bram were joined by family and close friends, among them Ouma Steyn. As Bram put the ring on Molly's finger, the household servants burst into song.

In Johannesburg they settled down to married life, both of them at the age of 29. Their flat on the Westcliff ridge had views stretching northwards to the Magaliesberg mountains. Then the following year, with the aid of a family bequest, they purchased a plot of land in Oaklands, a new part of the northern suburbs of Johannesburg, and commissioned the architect Norman Eaton to design a double-storey house. They moved there in April 1939. The spacious walled garden Molly created included saplings of *witstinkhout* brought from Abraham Fischer's old farm at Hillandale.

As well as his legal work, Bram renewed his links with the Joint Council, tackling a range of issues affecting the African population, such as pass laws, property rights and segregation measures. In 1936 he was elected to the executive of the Council, sitting alongside leading liberals. He helped formulate its response to government proposals to strip African voters from the common roll in the Cape Province and restrict them to a separate roll which allowed them to vote for white representatives to speak in parliament on their behalf. The proposals, said the Joint Council, would lead to the 'grave embitterment of race relations'. Bram and other Joint Council leaders addressed protest meetings in black townships in the Johannesburg area. But their views had no effect on the government, either on this issue or any other.

Bram soon moved in a more radical direction. He was particularly influenced by a conversation he had with Edwin Mofutsanyana, a prominent figure in both the Communist Party and the African National Congress, while driving him home one night to the west of Johannesburg:

I propounded to him the well-worn theory that if you separate races you diminish the points at which friction between them may occur and hence ensure good relations. His answer was the essence of simplicity. If you place the races of one country in two camps, he said, and cut off contact between them, those in each camp begin to forget that those in the other are ordinary human beings, that each lives and laughs in the same way, that each experiences joy or sorrow, pride or humiliation for the same reasons. Thereby each becomes suspicious of the other and each eventually fears the other, which is the basis of all racialism.

The growing menace of extremist Afrikaner groups added a new dimension. Hitler's rise to power in Germany and his theories of racial superiority had a marked influence on nationalist Afrikanerdom. Pro-Nazi groups like the Grey Shirts, the New Order and, above all, the *Ossewabrandwag*, which adopted the swastika badge, gave the Hitler salute, staged paramilitary rallies and threatened death to the Jews, gained an increasing following. DF Malan's 'purified' National Party was at the forefront of the anti-Semitic campaign, demanding a ban on Jewish immigration. Bram was horrified by the growing clamour for race superiority, believing that it would lead to disaster for South Africa as surely as it would do in Europe.

Disillusioned with the efforts of white liberals, Bram was increasingly drawn towards the Communist Party. Its history in South Africa had been tortuous. Formed in 1921 by a group consisting mainly of foreign-born British radicals and Eastern European Jews, it had found itself the following year supporting an insurrection by white mineworkers on the Witwatersrand determined to protect job segregation and block all African competition. Not until the late 1920s did the party attract a significant African membership. Then in 1928 the Communist International, having previously paid scant attention to its South African offspring, created turmoil by deciding that the task of the party in South Africa was to work for the establishment of an 'Independent Native Republic' as the first stage towards a workers' and peasants' government. Many white members saw this as racism in reverse and resigned. Others were drawn into a protracted period of purges and internal strife. By the early 1930s, the party had been reduced to an insignificant rump of 150 members, almost all of them white. But with the rise of fascist movements in the late 1930s, its fortunes revived once more. A new generation of political activists was attracted to its ranks.

What the Communist Party had to offer was not just a sense of political purpose, its vision of a socialist future, but an avenue through the racial barriers that shaped South African society. It was the only political organisation in South Africa not to practise some form of colour bar. It facilitated friendship across the colour line, giving many people their first glimpse of a multiracial world. The leadership remained largely in white hands. White communists were accustomed to playing a leading role both as teachers of theory and organisers in the field; their financial and professional resources gave them inherent advantages. Many were middle-class activists brought up in an anti-fascist tradition at a time when battles with pro-Nazi groups on the steps of Johannesburg City Hall were a regular event; a high proportion came from Jewish families. But the new membership of the Communist Party was predominantly African, impressed by its night schools, social gatherings and the prospect of a socialist future. Young Indian activists too played a significant part.

Bram was attracted both by the humanitarian ideals which under-pinned the communist faith and by the Marxist creed. He came to regard Marxism as a science, providing not only an explanation for the world's conflicts but a solution. Communism for him became a cause, one for which he had long searched and one from which he was never to waver; and with it went an unswerving loyalty to its originator, the Soviet Union.

A young activist, Miriam Hepner, met him at this time, soon after she joined the party in 1938. A lawyer working for an industrial council in Johannesburg, she collected funds for the party in her spare time and had been given Bram's name as a possible donor. She found him to be 'very charming and very sincere' and quite ready to donate ten shillings a month to party funds. Whenever she called at his chambers to collect the money, they would settle down for a chat about the Soviet Union, the rise of Nazism in Europe, and the threat from pro-Nazi groups in South Africa.

At the outbreak of war between Britain and Germany in 1939, Bram made his commitment clear. When General Smuts's government aligned South Africa with Britain, Bram followed the Communist Party line. The war, he argued, was an 'imperialist' war, not a war against fascism. It was being fought between the ruling classes of Britain and Germany for domination in Europe and colonial territories in Africa and Asia. It was a war about trade and investment, raw materials and markets. It was a capitalist war to which he was adamantly opposed.

Molly shared his commitment. She also believed that joining the Communist Party gave their lives a fuller meaning and a larger sense of purpose. The bonds they had forged in marriage now became the foundation of a remarkable partnership in politics.

CHAPTER 3

WAR AND APARTHEID

The 'real' war for Bram began when German troops invaded the Soviet Union in June 1941, threatening the home of socialism itself. Suddenly, the 'imperialist' war became a people's war. Communists emerged as enthusiastic supporters of the war effort, organising a series of 'Defend South Africa' rallies which carried the party's name and message to a wide audience. With tireless energy, Bram and Molly threw themselves into a host of activities to aid the Soviet war effort and to rally public support for the Soviet Union, making speeches, giving lectures, raising funds, organising fêtes and jumble sales. They both played key roles in organisations like the Friends of the Soviet Union, Medical Aid for Russia, and the Left Club. Bram spoke at rallies on the steps of the Johannesburg City Hall, addressed meetings of servicemen, lectured students, distributed leaflets at factory gates, and helped with street collections for the pro-Soviet weekly news-paper, *The Guardian*, staffed mainly by communists. He even volun-teered his services to the army but was turned down on health grounds, because of troubles with ulcers and high blood pressure.

Once the Soviet Union had joined the Allied war effort, public support for its struggle against Nazi Germany grew in leaps and bounds. Respectable figures like the minister of justice, Colin Steyn, the son of the old Orange Free State president, signed up as patrons to pro-Soviet organisations. Circulation of *The Guardian* soared to 50 000. Hundreds of new members were attracted to the Communist Party. In parliamentary elections in 1943, party candidates, though failing to win a seat, collected in all some 7 000 votes. The following year, in municipal elections, a party member, Hilda Bernstein, became the first and only communist candidate ever elected to public office in Johannesburg by an all-white electorate, winning the Hillbrow seat on the city council. Both Bram and Molly were involved in the campaign.

29

They also organised a fund-raising dance for *The Guardian* at their Beaumont Street house, turning it into an annual event.

Bram continued as well to campaign for African rights. He served on the Alexandra Health Committee, an administrative body attempting to improve conditions in Alexandra, a crime-ridden slum nine miles north of the city centre. When Alexandra's residents staged a bus boycott in protest against increases in fares to central Johannesburg, walking in their thousands each day to the city and back, Bram was in the thick of efforts to work out a solution.

He was also asked by the African National Congress, a small political organisation which had campaigned for African rights since 1912, for help in drawing up a new constitution. The ANC's leader, Alfred Xuma, a medical doctor who served with Bram on the Alexandra Health Committee, wanted to modernise the organisation and believed a new constitution would instil fresh momentum. It was duly introduced in 1943.

All this was in addition to a growing volume of legal work. Despite his overt communist connections, Bram remained highly valued by mining companies for his expertise on mining law, and much admired in the legal profession. In December 1942 he was elected to the Johannesburg Bar Council, serving without a break for the next ten years. His father, Percy, who himself had been elevated to the post of Judge-President of the Orange Free State, wrote to congratulate him – 'a wonderful sign of appreciation from your colleagues, especially with the number of votes you received'.

Bram also took up a post as lecturer in law at the University of the Witwatersrand, one of four English-speaking universities which permitted blacks to attend specialist courses. It was there in 1943 that he met a 24-year-old law student, Nelson Mandela, the only African in his class. Mandela was soon in need of Bram's professional services. After boarding a tram to get from the university campus to central Johannesburg one day, Mandela and three Indian friends fell into an altercation with a white conductor who shouted at the Indians that they were not allowed 'to carry a kaffir'. The conductor stopped the tram and called a policeman, who arrested the Indians 'for carrying a kaffir and disturbing the conductor in his duty'. All four were escorted to Marshall Square police station. Ordered to appear in court the next day, the students sought help from Bram who agreed to act as their advocate. In court, the magistrate greeted Bram warmly, mentioning that he had just returned from the Orange Free State where he had had the honour to meet Fischer's father, the Judge-President. The accused were quickly acquitted.

The toll on family life of all this activity was considerable. Working up to 18 hours a day, six or seven days a week, spending few evenings at home and constantly willing to help those in difficulty, like Mandela and his friends, Bram saw little of his two daughters, Ruth, born in 1939 and Ilse, born in 1943.

Molly was as keen an activist as he was, devoting much time to welfare schemes for African children. In 1945 she stood for election to the Johannesburg City Council as a Communist Party candidate, campaigning vigorously for better local facilities. An election leaflet she produced showed a photograph of two angelic young girls – Ruth and Ilse – with the caption: *'Beveilig Hulle Toekoms'* – 'Safeguard Their Future'. Even when the campaign was under way, she was still involved in a host of other activities. Writing to Bram's parents, she explained how 'running one jumble sale, one dance and one raffle and assisting with one fête, one Left Club and one straightforward collection', as well as campaigning for votes, had left her feeling quite exhausted. At the poll, she gained 461 votes but came last among the four candidates.

Bram, meanwhile, rose to the higher echelons of the Communist Party. As well as serving on the Johannesburg district committee, he was elected in 1945 to the party's central committee. A photograph taken at a party conference that year shows him standing among his colleagues, a slight figure dressed in a white open-necked shirt and jacket, wearing spectacles with round lenses and thin metal frames, looking confident and assured.

When the party launched a series of raids on shopkeepers to force them to abandon black-market price increases and sell goods at controlled prices, Bram could be seen with a crowbar in his hand opening boxes of soap to sell to customers, before handing the correct money to the shopkeeper.

Along with other communists he was caught up also in the African mineworkers' strike of 1946, the biggest labour protest in South

Africa's history. Party members had played a leading role in launching the African Mineworkers Union in 1941 – its president, JB Marks, was a Moscow-trained party organiser – and they were at the forefront in campaigning for improved wages and conditions. Most mineworkers were migrant labourers living in primitive barracks, sleeping on narrow shelves, cut off from all family and social life for months on end, and paid meagre wages. After sporadic strikes in 1943, a government commission of inquiry recommended substantial improvements. But three years later wages in the mines were less than half the minimum amount advocated by the commission, and employers ignored further demands from mineworkers.

When the African Mineworkers Union called a strike of all Africans employed in the gold mines, communist volunteers mobilised all their resources to support it. No previous attempt had been made to organise an industry-wide strike. With 45 mines strung out along 50 miles of the Witwatersrand, often in isolated areas surrounded by unused scrubland and constantly patrolled by mine police, the strike call far outstretched the capacity of union organisers. With revolutionary fervour, the communists provided teams of volunteers, cars, typewriters, duplicators and leaflet-writers. The party's district committee met secretly at different venues both by day and by night, directing its members' work. Leaflets were printed and distributed from end to end of the Witwatersrand. Flying squads of communist activists rushed from mine to mine to back up the efforts of the union.

The strike lasted for five days, drawing in some 70 000 miners, about a quarter of the African labour force. Nine mines came to a standstill, and production at ten others was disrupted. An increasingly ugly struggle developed between militant miners and police called in to break the strike, resulting in the death of 12 miners and injuries to more than 1 200 others. A Johannesburg newspaper reported how a force of 400 policemen, sent 1 000 feet underground at the Nigel gold mine to deal with 1 000 miners staging a sit-down strike, 'drove the natives up, stope by stope, level by level, until they reached the surface'. Police also raided the union's office in Johannesburg and the Communist Party's district office in Commissioner Street, removing caseloads of documents.

Determined to show that it could deal with 'the red menace',

General Smuts's government ordered the arrest of the entire Johannesburg district committee and other strike organisers, a total of 52 people, on charges of conspiracy to commit sedition.

Bram missed most of the action. When the strike started, he was on holiday in a wildlife reserve with Molly and the two girls, not expecting such a dramatic turn of events. As soon as he heard the news he rushed back to Johannesburg, but by the time he arrived the strike was virtually over. Nevertheless, he insisted on standing trial with his colleagues.

The accused were eventually charged with assisting a strike which was illegal in terms of war measures still in force. Bram pleaded guilty along with all the others, not because of his involvement in the strike, he said, but because he wished to associate himself with the actions of the district committee. Most of the accused were given suspended fines.

The repercussions from the strike were nevertheless severe. The mineworkers union was virtually destroyed. The communists too found themselves the target of harassment. Police raids were carried out on party premises, on the office of *The Guardian*, and on the houses of prominent officials. Eight members of the central committee in Cape Town were charged anew with sedition. The evidence was flimsy, but the proceedings dragged on for two years. The popular support that the communists had enjoyed during the war soon evaporated.

In 1948 a far greater threat emerged when Daniel Malan's National Party was swept to power on a surge of Afrikaner nationalism. Its aim was to ensure white supremacy for all time through a policy of apartheid and to destroy the black peril, the *swart gevaar*, it said white society faced. New laws were introduced prohibiting interracial sex and marriage, and the new government made it clear that it would extend racial separation to every facet of life – residence, amenities, transport, education and politics.

Amongst its targets was the Communist Party. Almost immediately on taking power, Malan set up a commission to investigate the influence of communism in South Africa, and in 1949 the commission duly reported that the Communist Party represented a danger to 'our national life, our democratic institutions and our Western philosophy'.

The result the following year was a piece of legislation eventually called the *Suppression of Communism Act*, which gave the government powers to outlaw the Communist Party and deal with other opponents it deemed to be troublesome. So wide was the Act's definition of communism that it could be used to silence anyone who opposed government policy simply by 'naming' them. Communism was now defined to mean not only Marxist-Leninism but also 'any related form of that doctrine' which sought to bring about 'any political, industrial, social or economic change within the Union by the promotion of disturbance or disorder' or which aimed at 'the encouragement of feelings of hostility between the European and non-European races of the Union'.

In effect, the Act equated communism with any determined form of opposition to apartheid. The government was empowered to ban any organisation, to remove its members from public office, to place them under house arrest, to restrict their movements, and to prohibit them from attending public or even social gatherings. No reasons had to be given in 'naming' communists; nor was there any right of appeal. Such action, moreover, could be taken against anyone who had ever professed communism.

Before the Act took effect, Bram travelled to Cape Town in June to attend a meeting of central committee members called to debate whether they should continue their work underground. The difficulties of moving from legal work to illegal work without a pause were known to be considerable. The police were already in possession of membership lists, seized during raids on party offices. Attempts to create the skeleton of an underground organisation had already failed. Bram was in favour of disbanding the party. So were most other members present; only two voted for an underground existence.

On 20 June, four days before the Act became law, Sam Kahn, a Communist Party member of parliament elected by voters from the African roll, announced the party's dissolution. Many communists, however, remained politically active. African members, numbering about 1 600 at the time, were able to channel their energies into the African National Congress. Indian members found a similar home in the Indian Congresses. The 150 white members lacked an immediate base from which to operate, but it was not long before they were to regroup and continue to work underground.

34

CHAPTER 4

BEAUMONT STREET

As year by year the tentacles of apartheid reached ever deeper into South African society, the Fischer household at number 12 Beaumont Street became an oasis for friends and acquaintances of all races determined to keep alive the idea of a multiracial world. The Fischers were renowned for their hospitality, welcoming visitors at all hours. Beaumont Street was a regular venue for jumble sales, fund-raising events and children's parties. On the veranda, political discussion went on hour after hour. On summer weekends, friends flocked to the swimming pool. At the annual dances for *The Guardian*, up to 200 guests would arrive. There were even celebrations to mark the anniversary of the Russian revolution. From the kitchen, Molly would provide an endless flow of food and refreshments. In a letter to Bram's parents, she once described how on a hot weekend the swimming pool resembled the beach at Muizenberg, a popular resort near Cape Town, at the height of the season. 'It's all very interesting,' she said, 'but sometimes I long for a rainy Sunday.'

To all comers, Bram was invariably warm and approachable. 'He was deeply interested in people, in what they said and what they did,' recalled his friend Hilda Bernstein. 'He was concerned about people's lives, about their families. He had an instinct for bringing people together.' Bram was particularly admired for his willingness to help with other people's problems. 'He had an enormous compassion for other people,' recalled Rusty Bernstein. 'He was driven to do good. He would work himself to a standstill.'

He was also known for his modest and courteous nature. Nelson Mandela remembered him as 'a humble person, self-effacing, almost retiring'. Walter Sisulu, another leading African politician, described him as 'a perfect gentleman', widely liked and trusted. 'His manner made it difficult for people to say no.' Despite his strong political convictions, Bram never attempted to impose his ideas on others, nor even to proselytise. 'He never tried to throw his weight about, to try to recruit somebody to his point of view,' said Mandela. 'I can hardly recall an occasion when I had a conversation about ideology with him. He would never start a conversation on things of that nature.' Even in his dealings with the police, Bram remained polite and dignified, however fraught the circumstances, earning their respect. 'He treated every individual with the same gentle courtesy,' recalled Hilda Bernstein.

Yet beneath this calm, unassuming exterior lay an iron resolve. Bram was a true believer in communism and in the Soviet Union, and held fast to his faith with religious zeal. Nothing deflected him from it, neither doubts nor uncertainties. Whatever twists and turns were required to follow the Soviet line, Bram made them unhesitatingly. Unfavourable reports about Stalin's regime he dismissed as propaganda put about by the Western press. When Krushchev subsequently denounced Stalin for his crimes, Bram acknowledged the reality of them, but his loyalty to the Soviet Union was unshaken. The overriding cause of communism remained his lodestar. He followed it with a passion that never diminished.

Molly, by comparison, had a sharper personality. Her outlook was more cynical. Unlike Bram, she enjoyed making the odd caustic remark. 'Molly was outspoken,' said Walter Sisulu. 'Unlike other communists, you could argue with her.' Mandela, too, found her impressive. 'Molly was more aggressive than Bram and very warm in her personality.' Her commitment to the cause, however, was no less determined than Bram's, and through all the trials and tribulations that lay ahead she remained the anchor of his life.

By outward appearances, the Fischer family led a fairly conventional middle-class existence, enjoying a comfortable house in the northern suburbs, a spacious garden with a swimming pool, several servants in their employ, and regular holidays to the coast and in wildlife reserves. Bram's standing in the legal profession continued to grow. In November 1951 he was appointed a senior advocate, a King's Counsel, by the Nationalist minister of justice, Charles Swart, fondly known to the Fischers and others as 'Oom Blackie', a Free State lawyer who in his youth had participated in the 1914 rebellion. 'I congratulate you on your admission to senior status as an advocate,' wrote Oom Blackie. 'I also wish you success in your further career at the Bar.'

Bram replied:

It was friendly of you to congratulate me on my appointment as KC. I value it highly. The disadvantage of the recognition is that if one does not succeed in the elevated status, the 'appointer' – the Minister – cannot be held responsible! But whether I succeed or not, I hope nevertheless that I shall always be able to exert myself to maintain the high traditions of our profession.

Family life was also fairly conventional. Bram and Molly kept in close touch with their parents, making frequent trips to Bergendal and to Silverton. The two girls, Ruth and Ilse, were sent to all-white Anglican schools. If anything, Ruth felt her father was too conservative. Bram insisted on strict rules about manners and etiquette. He disapproved of sitting on the pavement, eating in the street, wearing lipstick and chewing gum. 'I was very aware of having to behave according to the rules,' Ruth recalled. At school events, the girls were invariably embarrassed when Bram appeared wearing khaki trousers and speaking Afrikaans. Their brother, Paul, born in 1947, was also sent to an elite private school in Johannesburg, St John's.

Apart from the rules of behaviour, there was usually a sense of fun about Bram. He delighted in organising picnics and birthday parties and visits to bird sanctuaries and fishing expeditions. 'He laughed a lot,' recalled Hilda Bernstein. 'He was not a deadly serious sort of person.' The Fischer children were brought up to enjoy themselves. Ruth recalled: 'He taught one the fact that life was to be made fun of, which I think is quite a rare quality for one of those politicos. They were pretty intense.' A young friend of the Fischer family, Pat Davidson, who often went on holiday with them, remembered Bram's ability to mix easily with children, to keep them interested with stories and games. 'He had a lovely twinkle in his eye, a laugh in his voice. He smiled a lot.'

Yet from an early stage the Fischer children knew that their parents were different. During the 1948 election campaign, when Ruth wanted to know for which party they would be voting, so that she could tell her school friends, Molly explained that they would vote for the Communist Party, but that it would be better to tell her friends that it was the opposition United Party. Bram and Molly also made it clear that they were atheists, though they had no objection to the Christian upbringing their children received at school. Most unusual of all was the Fischers' decision to take into the household a young African girl, Nora Mlambo, a niece of one of their servants whose own mother had died and who was much the same age as Ilse. Nora shared a room with Ilse and was treated as a member of the family.

There were, too, early clouds over family life. From childhood, Paul had suffered from a chronic cough and he was soon diagnosed as having cystic fibrosis, a genetic disease which resulted in the lungs filling up with a sticky, immovable mucus. Often the only effective treatment was to let his head hang over the edge of the bed and to beat him on the back to loosen the mucus in his lungs. He was at first expected to survive for only about six years, but stubbornly he hung on. Then at the age of eight he developed diabetes and needed regular insulin injections; two years later he underwent a major operation for a stomach obstruction. His life became a routine of diet calculations and urine checks and efforts to stem the unrelenting fits of coughing.

Bram and Molly worked hard to give him as normal a life as possible, encouraging him to participate in sports at school. At primary school he played soccer for the 'A' team, competed in athletic sports, and sang in the choir. 'We're always so glad,' wrote Molly, 'if he can just feel that he's not any different from other boys.' In the face of such handicaps, Paul showed an indomitable spirit and developed a dry wit. But there was always the fear that his life would suddenly be cut short.

The tumult of political life meanwhile swirled about them. Among the groups opposing apartheid, there were liberals, communists, Trotskyists, Africanists, African nationalists, Indian and Coloured organisations, and assorted churchmen. All were determined to resist the onslaught of apartheid, but some spent as much time attacking one another as they spent attacking the government.

Liberals and communists fought a running battle lasting for years. There was also a prolonged feud between Africanists and communists. Africanists accused communists of trying to use the African nationalist movement for their own ends. They distrusted the prominent role that whites played in communist politics and the emphasis that communists placed on class struggle rather than racial oppression. What the Africanists wanted was to assert an African identity, to give Africans control of their own future, to use African political power to change South African society.

At the forefront of the Africanist campaign was the youth wing of the African National Congress, the Congress Youth League, launched in 1944 by a group of young activists, including Nelson Mandela, Walter Sisulu and Oliver Tambo, with the aim of driving the ANC in a more radical direction. The slogans favoured by the more extreme Africanists included 'Africa for the Africans' and 'Hurl the white man to the sea', which they tried to get the ANC's annual conference in Bloemfontein in 1945 to accept. Mandela was sympathetic to their views: 'While I was not prepared to hurl the white man into the sea,' he said, 'I would have been perfectly happy if he climbed aboard his steamships and left the continent of his own volition.'

The communists were viewed with similar hostility. In 1945, in an overt attempt to rid the ANC of Communist Party members, the Youth League put forward a motion proposing that members with dual allegiance to other organisations should be expelled from the ANC. Its 'Basic Policy', drawn up in 1948, warned of 'the need for vigilance against communists and other groups which foster non-African interests ... groups which seek to impose on our struggle cut-and-dried formulas, which so far from clarifying the issues of our struggle, only serve to obscure the fundamental fact that we are oppressed not as a class but as a people'.

The help of white liberals was dismissed as worthless. 'Their voice is negligible, and in the last analysis counts for nothing. In their struggle for freedom the Africans will be wasting their time and deflecting their forces if they look up to the Europeans either for inspiration or for help.' Indian organisations were given similarly short shrift. What the Youth League essentially wanted was to 'go it alone'.

The main body of the ANC was meanwhile moving in a different direction, seeking new links with other opposition groups facing the menace of apartheid. Some leading figures in the Youth League also began to change their minds. Among them was Walter Sisulu who had come to accept that Africanism, however appealing at an emotional level, from a strategic point of view had obvious limitations. Elected as the ANC's general secretary in 1948, he encouraged a broader approach to the business of opposition.

Mandela, however, held firm to his Africanist beliefs. Though he had a wide and varied circle of friends, including many communists, he continued to attack all suggestion of collaboration with other groups, whether white, Indian or communist. When the communists initiated plans for a one-day strike in 1950 in protest against the government's moves to introduce the *Suppression of Communism Act*, Mandela and other Youth League members took to breaking up Communist Party meetings, heckling speakers and tearing up placards.

But the influence of a number of his communist friends eventually began to leave its mark. The impression that Bram in particular made on him was profound, as much on a personal level as a political one. 'His whole character, his demeanour really impressed me tremendously,' said Mandela. 'You assessed his attitude not from what he said but the way he treated his workers – his gardener, a maid, a black child he adopted.'

Their friendship became increasingly important. 'Bram was a unifying factor with the others around him, a peacemaker. You wouldn't find him at meetings going all out against anybody. He was a diplomat who received the support of everyone he worked with.' Above all, there was Bram's steadfast support for African rights. 'Bram's commitment to the struggle helped to change many of us in the ANC from being Africanists to believers in non-racial democracy.' What was especially important in influencing Mandela's own outlook was that Bram was an Afrikaner. In an age when Afrikaners were coming to be regarded by Africans as the enemy, Mandela had found an Afrikaner friend.

In the first major protest against apartheid laws, Africans and Indians joined forces in June 1952 to mount a 'Defiance Campaign'. The plan was that trained volunteers would deliberately court arrest and imprisonment by contravening selected laws and regulations like using railway coaches, waiting rooms and platform seats designated for Europeans only, or by parading on the streets after curfew without permits, or by entering African locations without approval. The idea had originally been proposed by Walter Sisulu in the hope that it would force the government to introduce reforms. The campaign attracted widespread support, transforming the ANC from a small elite group into a mass movement. Over five months, nearly 8 000 volunteers went to prison for periods ranging from one to three weeks.

But far from conceding reforms, the government reacted with ruthless determination to crush the campaign. Twenty leaders, including Sisulu and Mandela, were arrested and charged with promoting communism. Their trial in November 1952 became the focus of national attention. For the first time in 40 years, ANC leaders faced the prospect of imprisonment for political protest against the government.

Bram was asked to join the team of defence lawyers. Much depended on the meaning of communism in terms of the law. Trying to interpret the *Suppression of Communism Act*, Judge Franz Rumpff asked the prosecutor 'whether a party of European women who sat down in the street and refused to leave when ordered to do so because they had decided on a plan to obtain a change in regard to the rules of jury service, would be guilty of communism?' The prosecutor replied: 'The scope of the Act is very wide.' In his verdict, Judge Rumpff found the accused guilty of what was termed 'statutory communism', but added, 'This has nothing to do with communism as it is commonly known.' He gave the accused suspended sentences. In future years, Bram was to become only too familiar with arguments in court about what constituted communism.

The communist fraternity had meanwhile been active in other areas. Largely through Bram's efforts, a Transvaal Peace Council was launched in 1951 and a South African Peace Council in 1953, both of which were affiliated to the pro-Soviet World Peace Council established in Paris in 1949. It was as a representative of the Transvaal Peace Council that Bram travelled to Vienna in November 1952 to attend a Congress of the Peoples for Peace, where anti-colonial and anti-imperial rhetoric constituted a large part of the agenda. Delegates from Korea, Vietnam, Malaya, Algeria and Morocco spoke of the suffering and hardship of their peoples. Bram added a South African voice, referring to the poverty and 'voicelessness' of the black population. On his return in January 1953 he addressed meeting after meeting on his experiences there, and took a leading role in the newly-formed South African Society for Peace and Friendship with the Soviet Union.

But the communists' main efforts were concentrated on regrouping underground. In 1953, in conditions of utmost secrecy, a small working group of senior figures began to reconstitute the party, building up a new network of cells. As well as Bram, the group included Yusuf Dadoo, the Indian communist leader, Moses Kotane, a Moscow-trained party organiser, Michael Harmel, a leading theoretician, and Rusty Bernstein, a propaganda expert. The party's founding conference was held at the back of an Indian trader's store in a village on the East Rand to which many delegates were taken in closed vehicles without knowing their destination.

Their numbers were small – fewer than 100 members were at the core of Communist Party activity, most of them living in the Transvaal. They operated mainly in small units of four or five people, meeting clandestinely, often in 'unmarked' cars owned by friends and colleagues or in 'safe' houses. Among white communists, as well as Bram and Molly, there were a number of notable husband-and-wife teams: Rusty and Hilda Bernstein, Jack and Rica Hodgson, Joe Slovo and Ruth First, Brian and Sonya Bunting, Ben and Mary Turok, and Eli and Violet Weinberg. In addition to cell meetings, party members often spent time in one another's company. Beaumont Street was a regular venue for the Bernsteins, the Hodgsons, the Slovos and the Weinbergs. Michael Harmel went there three or four times a week and tended to stay late. Moses Kotane was another frequent visitor. Although most members, like Bram, were readily identified as being 'former' communists, their involvement in a well-organised, tightly-disciplined, underground version of the Communist Party was never suspected. Meetings of the secretariat took place several times each week. National conferences were also held, with delegates attending from towns across South Africa, without attracting the attention of the police Special Branch.

The communists were particularly adept at keeping alive a radical press. When *The Guardian* was suppressed by the government in 1952, a new paper, *The Clarion*, appeared the following week, using the same staff and the same editor. A dance was held at Beaumont Street in April 1953 to raise funds for the 'new' paper. When *The Clarion* was suppressed, *People's World* appeared; after that came *Advance* and then *New Age*, at which point the government tired of the game. The papers all devoted considerable space to descriptions of Soviet achievements and justifications of Soviet foreign policy. Ivan Schermbrucker, one of Bram's closest friends and a grandson of a member of the Cape legislature, ran the Johannesburg office.

Their main energy, however, was channelled into a new organisation, the Congress of Democrats, which they launched in 1953 as a white counterpart to the African National Congress and the Indian Congress. Not all its members were communists, but communists played a key role in its foundation and in its leadership ranks. Once again it was Bram who was instrumental in getting it off the ground. But a few weeks before its inaugural conference in Johannesburg, his involvement was cut short when he was served with two orders under the *Suppression of Communism Act* prohibiting him from attending any public gathering for two years and banning him from membership of a range of organisations including the Congress of Democrats and the South African Peace Council.

Beaumont Street now became a regular target for police surveillance. In July 1953 the first police raid took place, with Special Branch detectives searching for documents and pamphlets. In its determination to crush opposition, the Nationalist government turned the Special Branch into a political arm, separate from the rest of the police force, giving it licence to act as it saw fit in dealing with political dissidents. Special Branch detectives tapped phone calls, intercepted mail, bugged meetings, kept activists under constant surveillance, and used threats and intimidation with their employers and families. They regularly invaded meetings, recording speeches, photographing members of the audience and noting car number plates. The Special Branch was directly responsible for making recommendations about banning orders and other methods of putting dissidents 'out of action'. The activists in turn delighted in trying to outwit Special Branch detectives, regarding most of them as being inept and incompetent. Yet, however inefficient the Special Branch may have been, it represented an ever-present danger.

Molly was eventually ensnared in the same net. Like Bram, she had been involved in a host of organisations, including the Congress of Democrats and the South African Society for Peace and Friendship with the Soviet Union. Along with her friend Violet Weinberg, she was also active in a Communist Party cell that regularly met on a park bench in The Wilds in Johannesburg. As a member of the Federation of South African Women, she had attended ceremonies marking the fifth anniversary of the Chinese revolution in October 1954, and spent five months travelling abroad, visiting not only China but the Soviet Union and East Germany. A month after her return she, like Bram, was banned from attending all public gatherings and from membership of a score of organisations.

Their banning orders meant that neither of them was able to participate overtly in preparations for holding a national convention of anti-apartheid groups called the Congress of the People. The idea had first been proposed by the ANC as a way of reviving mass political activity. Other organisations, including the Indian Congress, the Coloured People's Organisation and the Congress of Democrats, were then invited to join in. The main task of the Congress was to draw up a Freedom Charter to point the road ahead to a multiracial society. Teams of 'freedom volunteers' were recruited to canvass support and to collect suggestions for what the Freedom Charter might contain.

Members of the Congress of Democrats were notably energetic during the preparations for the Congress, raising fears among Africanists within the ANC that left-wing whites were trying to manipulate events for their own purposes. The newly-formed Liberal Party, launched by whites in 1953 to act as a multiracial opposition group, declined to participate mainly because of the prominent involvement of Congress of Democrats members.

Behind the scenes, the influence of Congress of Democrats members was even more crucial than their critics suspected. Most of the burden of writing the draft version of the Freedom Charter was undertaken by Rusty Bernstein, secretly a member of the Communist Party's central committee. The economic clause of the Charter, which demanded the nationalisation of the banks and 'monopoly industry', was largely the work of Ben Turok, another active Communist Party member.

The Congress of the People duly opened on 25 June 1955 on a rough football field near Kliptown, a ramshackle collection of houses and shacks 15 miles to the south-west of Johannesburg. Nearly 3 000 delegates attended – lawyers, doctors, clergymen, city workers and peasants – including 320 Indians, 230 Coloureds and 112 whites, a multiracial gathering unique in South Africa's history. Like other banned activists, Bram and Molly watched from a distance, taking Ruth with them.

Presiding over the occasion was Piet Beyleveld, the first president of the Congress of Democrats, an Afrikaner trade unionist whom Bram recruited into the Communist Party and who was later to betray him. Clause by clause the Freedom Charter was read out and approved by a show of hands. On the second day, when only two sections were left, the proceedings were abruptly interrupted by armed police who surrounded the delegates. Senior officers mounted the platform and presented Beyleveld with a warrant to investigate treason. He then explained to delegates the reasons for the police action, told them he had authorised the removal of all papers and documents, and asked if they wished to proceed with the Congress. The crowd roared their assent. While police worked their way up and down the rows of delegates, searching bags, confiscating documents, recording names and addresses, and taking photographs, speakers on the platform resumed reading out the Freedom Charter.

It was a document that became the subject of endless controversy, though much of its content was relatively modest. The Freedom Charter affirmed the right of all citizens to vote, to hold office and to be equal before the law. It promised equal status for 'all national groups' and an end to discriminatory legislation. 'South Africa,' it declared, 'belongs to all who live in it, black and white.' It went on to state that the mines, banks and monopoly industry would be transferred to public ownership and that land would be redistributed. Other promises concerned free compulsory education, minimum wages, free medical care, and welfare for the aged. The tone throughout was idealistic, at times naïve. 'Rent and prices should be lowered, food plentiful and no one shall go hungry,' the Freedom Charter proclaimed. 'Slums shall be demolished, and new suburbs built.' No suggestions were put forward as to how all this would be achieved.

In the South African context, however, such statements were dangerous. White liberals deplored the 'socialist' character of the Freedom Charter, arguing that left-wing activists in the Congress of Democrats had clearly got the upper hand, thus justifying their refusal to take part. Africanist critics within the ANC were outraged by the clause declaring that South Africa belonged to 'all who live in it, black and white'. In the Africanist view, the only true 'owners' of South Africa were Africans.

In an article in Michael Harmel's left-wing journal, *Liberation*, Nelson Mandela rejected the notion that the Freedom Charter was 'a blueprint for a socialist state', but he was nevertheless forthright about the impact it would make: 'The Charter is more than a mere list of demands for democratic reform,' he wrote. 'It is a revolutionary document precisely because the changes it envisages cannot be won without breaking up the economic and political set-up of present South Africa.'

The government thought so too, and set out to prove that the Charter's aims could not be achieved without violence. In December 1956, police arrested 156 activists on charges of treason. Among them were almost all senior ANC leaders and a number of prominent white activists including Rusty Bernstein, Joe Slovo, Ruth First, Jack Hodgson, Piet Beyleveld and a British-born social worker, Helen Joseph. Despite the gravity of the charges, they were released on bail. For month after month the preparatory examination of their case dragged on in the Drill Hall in Johannesburg. Thousands of documents were produced; a succession of Special Branch detectives took the witness stand. Bram's name occasionally cropped up in the prosecution's evidence.

In December 1957, without any explanation, charges against 61 of the accused were dropped. Then in January 1958 the presiding magistrate decided that there was 'sufficient reason' for committing the remainder to trial in the Transvaal Supreme Court.

Bram was involved in the defence team as second-in-command to Issy Maisels, one of the most experienced and distinguished lawyers in South Africa. The two advocates made a sharp contrast. Maisels, a tall, bespectacled figure, with dark hair receding from a massive forehead, was a former major in the South African Air Force and chairman of the Johannesburg Bar. He was not a 'political' advocate accustomed to political trials; he undertook to lead the defence case on the condition that it was conducted on a legal basis, not a political basis. His style was to cut a swathe through the prosecutor's case.

Bram was short and stocky, but even in middle age retained a gentle, almost boyish face, though his hair was turning grey. His quiet demeanour, his courteous, soft-spoken nature gave little clue as to the complex life he led. Occasionally there were flashes of deep anger, when his face turned red, but they rarely surfaced. In court, his manner was self-effacing, hesitant, almost apologetic, but his research and preparation were invariably meticulous and he pursued his arguments with implacable determination. 'His is always the reasonable approach, the appeal to the rational,' recorded Helen Joseph, one of the accused. 'He is a master of persuasion, yet he can say the most deadly things in the most gentle way.' Nelson Mandela, a lawyer himself, spent months watching Bram at work. 'His skills as a lawyer were phenomenal,' he recalled. 'He was quietly efficient, humble, not given to any form of confrontation. When others would be aggressive, he would be highly diplomatic and I appreciated that very much.'

Bram was particularly effective in dealing with state witnesses. 'He won the confidence of his witness with gentle skill,' recalled Helen Joseph. 'He didn't chase his witness into a corner and pin him down, indeed he never raised his voice, but in the end, somehow, the witness turned out to have said just what Bram wanted him to say. We marvelled at his unerring technique. I think the Crown [the prosecution] did too, when they realised the fatal concessions their witnesses were making so unsuspectingly.'

From the opening moments of the trial, held in what had once been Pretoria's Synagogue, the defence team gave the prosecution no quarter. Maisels opened with an assault on the indictment lasting nearly ten hours, arguing that it failed to provide in clear terms exactly what changes the accused had to meet. Bram followed with a four-hour attack on the indictment, making the same point about the lack of particulars. After weeks of argument, the prosecution abandoned the indictment altogether and was forced to start anew.

A huge party was held at the Slovos' house in Roosevelt Park that night to celebrate the event. Towards midnight the house was surrounded by police, who swarmed in through the doors and windows, hoping to catch blacks drinking illegal liquor. The blacks were well versed at this game, and not one was found with so much as a drop of liquor.

Not until August 1959 did the real trial begin. By then the number of accused on trial had been reduced to 30. This group, according to the prosecution, comprised the most 'dangerous'; they included Nelson Mandela and Walter Sisulu. The others, relegated to a 'second division' on suspended charges, included several leading figures in the underground Communist Party – Joe Slovo, Ruth First, Rusty Bernstein and Piet Beyleveld.

The prosecution's case centred on proving that the intention of the accused was to act violently. According to the prosecution, the accused knew that to achieve the demands of the Freedom Charter in their life-time inevitably meant 'a violent collision with the state resulting in its subversion'. It claimed that they were part of an international communist-inspired movement which was 'pledged to overthrow by violence all governments in non-communist countries where sections of the population did not have equal political and economic rights'.

Once again, thousands of documents were read into the record; once again, Special Branch detectives and expert witnesses trooped into the witness stand to give their testimony. Every piece of evidence, every speech, every document was picked over for signs of violent intent. The monotony was excruciating. When a mining company case came his way in March 1960, Bram said it was 'absolute heaven' to be working on something other than treason.

Outside the court, Bram was constantly engaged in trying to alleviate the problems that families of the accused encountered. He was also assiduous in organising dinner parties at Beaumont Street to introduce ANC leaders on trial to white politicians and businessmen, most of whom had never met Africans on a social basis. On one occasion, he invited Nelson Mandela along with the judges who were presiding at his trial. 'We never discussed the trial,' recalled Mandela, 'but it helped to introduce a particular respect by the judges afterwards.'

The prosecution finally closed its case on 10 March 1960. Four days later the defence case began. But the defence team had hardly got into their stride when a sudden upheaval occurred that brought the trial proceedings to a halt and shook the country to its core.

On 21 March, in Sharpeville, a black township in southern Trans-vaal, police opened fire indiscriminately on a crowd of several thousand Africans protesting against the pass laws, killing 67 and wounding 186 others. Most were shot in the back as they tried to flee.

The Sharpeville massacre became a permanent symbol of the brutality of the apartheid regime. Its impact was felt around the world, producing a storm of protest. Never before had South Africa faced such universal condemnation.

The ANC called on workers to stay at home and observe a day of mourning. The response in many large towns was overwhelming. In demonstrations across the country, thousands of Africans burned their pass books. Violence broke out in Johannesburg's black townships. In Cape Town, a massive throng of 30 000 Africans marched into the centre of the city to protest against police brutality in trying to break up a week-long strike there. Many blacks believed they were on the verge of liberation.

To much of the white population it seemed that South Africa had indeed reached a critical turning point. The sight of massed ranks of blacks marching on the centre of a white city suggested that black patience had finally snapped. As fear and alarm about the defiant mood of the black population spread, whites rushed to gun shops, clearing out their stocks. House prices and the stock market slumped. The outburst of international protest against the Sharpeville killings added to the atmosphere of crisis. Liberal whites were convinced that the government would have no alternative but to change its policies.

But far from being willing to make concessions, the government ordered a massive crackdown on its opponents. It introduced new security legislation, outlawed the African National Congress and its small rival, the Pan-Africanist Congress, declared a state of emergency, and ordered the arrest of hundreds of anti-apartheid dissidents. On the list of addresses to be raided was Beaumont Street.

CHAPTER 5

STATE OF EMERGENCY

It was two o'clock in the morning when the door bell rang. Expecting it would be the Special Branch, Molly went downstairs to the door to give Bram a few minutes of extra time. But the police had come for Molly, not for Bram. 'It's all right, dear,' she called out, 'it's for me.' While the police searched the house, Molly went upstairs to pack. She was driven to Johannesburg's main prison, the Fort.

Molly had not been noticeably active at the time. She had been teaching at an Indian community school in Fordsburg, set up by Michael Harmel for pupils whose own school had been closed as part of the government's drive to remove the Indian population from areas of Johannesburg designated for white residents only. Otherwise her chief preoccupation had been caring for Paul. In her efforts to ease his plight, she had contacted medical experts around the world, developing a profound knowledge of the problems of cystic fibrosis.

But the Special Branch was determined to round up all dissidents on its lists. Because Bram's arrest would have disrupted proceedings at the treason trial, causing serious embarrassment, Molly alone went to prison. In the case of a number of families – the Bernsteins, the Weinbergs, the Buntings, the Heymanns – both partners were imprisoned, leaving children without parents.

Few managed to escape the dragnet. Joe Slovo was arrested, but Ruth First, disguised in a red wig, escaped with her three children to Swaziland. A few prominent figures, like Oliver Tambo and Yusuf Dadoo, the Indian communist leader, slipped away into exile. A small group of communists, including Michael Harmel and Moses Kotane, avoided arrest and continued to operate underground, moving from one hideout to another. But otherwise active opposition was obliterated. By the beginning of May, the total number of arrests had reached 18 000.

Bram's life became a hectic round of keeping abreast of the treason trial in Pretoria, holding Beaumont Street together, and dealing with a host of problems confronting the wives and families of detainees. 'During the emergency,' recalled Rusty Bernstein, 'Bram was undertaking everyone else's problems.' As Ruth was away in Cape Town studying at university, much of the burden of running Beaumont Street fell on Ilse, who was in her final year at school.

Inside the Fort, a former Boer fortress built in 1899 on a hill near the centre of Johannesburg to defend it against the British, Molly was detained in comfortable quarters in the old hospital section, in the company of many of her activist friends. They occupied themselves by organising French and maths classes, giving lectures and playing chess and Scrabble. One of her companions was Rica Hodgson, a glamorous figure with a Rita Hayworth hairstyle, famous for wearing tight-fitting skirts and stiletto high heels, who insisted on keeping up standards in prison. A dedicated communist, she made sure that her fellow detainees had their hair done every week, taught some of them how to use make-up, and manicured their nails. 'They all felt much better for it, you know,' Molly reported from prison. 'The standard of dress around here is pretty high.'

Despite the relative comfort, Molly's constant concern was for Paul. Each day he needed regular treatment for his lungs, as well as insulin injections and other medical dosages. He showed remarkable resilience in coping with his disabilities, managing to participate in cricket, swimming, athletics and other school activities. But Molly worried whether he could stand the pace. Once, after one of Paul's bad spells, Molly had told Bram: 'I always feel I would sell the house to get him relief for 24 hours.' In prison she talked about him obsessively. 'Molly was totally absorbed with Paul and his illness, with trying to keep him alive,' said her fellow detainee, Hilda Bernstein. 'It formed the background to her whole life.'

During prison visits, Molly always appeared cheerful. On Ilse's birthday, she presented her daughter with a bunch of violets picked from the prison garden, passing it through the wire mesh partition that separated them, with an accompanying poem which started:

What gift for a dear teenage daughter
Can a mother present her from gaol
Where shopping is strictly 'verboten'
And strictures and censors prevail ...

But as week after week of prison life dragged on, with no end in sight, it began to take its toll on the detainees.

At the treason trial, meanwhile, the defence team asked the court to adjourn on the grounds that the government, by declaring a state of emergency, had effectively made a judgement on the case. Moreover, they argued, defence witnesses would be fearful of giving testimony which might now lead to their prosecution under the terms of the emergency regulations.

The judges, however, after accepting assurances from the minister of justice of an indemnity for the witnesses, decided that the case could proceed. To make clear their protest against the conditions under which the trial was being held, the defendants, who were being held in prisons in Pretoria, announced that they would dispense with their defence lawyers. Maisels duly rose to tell the court: 'We have no further mandate and we will consequently not trouble your Lordships further.' All the defence lawyers then walked out, leaving the defendants to handle their own case.

In May, six weeks after the emergency was declared, the authorities decided to transfer white detainees in the Fort to prisons in Pretoria. The men went peaceably enough. But the women, furious at being removed even further from their families, refused to go, and each one of them had to be carried by prison staff to the vehicles taking them away. 'The jail authorities were terribly shaken,' recalled Joe Slovo, who was among the detainees waiting to leave in the police convoy. 'It was beyond their imagination that a group of seemingly respectable white women could engage in such unseemly physical defiance of authority.'

No sooner had they arrived in Pretoria than the women wrote to the minister of justice, threatening to go on hunger strike unless they were released. On Friday 13 May the strike duly began. Some of the men joined in. Helen Joseph, one of the defendants in the treason trial and by general agreement exempt from the strike, observed its progress day by day on her return from court. 'The women were excited over the first day of the hunger strike and were comparing degrees of hunger,' she recorded. 'Next morning, much discussion again on hunger, though most of the woman said they didn't feel hungry, only a bit headachey and light-headed.'

The following week, the effect began to tell:

They became slow and flagging and they didn't talk much. Knitting gradually ceased and the women didn't want to go down in the yard, for the physical effort of going down and getting back was very great. All activities were suspended and the sweeping and kitchen duties fell away – there was no food being prepared. As the women grew weaker, some of them took to their beds and just lay dozing, reading desultorily. But they were indomitable and none would be the first to give in. The wives were visited by their detained husbands, also on an indefinite strike. Interviews with the authorities were stormy but there were no outright efforts to force the women to give in. They lost many pounds in weight, just in this one week: those who were slim before looked emaciated and the heavy ones looked worse, for their flesh began to hang. And one and all they had a grey look to their faces. There was little laughter and the rare smiles were slow. They began to have almost the look of zombies ...

One morning, as I came from the bathroom block into the yard, I saw them almost crawling to the bathrooms as though they could hardly put one foot in front of the other ... It was a terrible and moving sight. No reply had come to their demand for release, after eight days of fasting, and yet they were committed to go on. And they wanted to go on; their spirit never weakened.

On the eighth day of the strike, a Saturday morning, a children's demonstration protesting against the detentions was held on the steps of the City Hall in Johannesburg. A group of about 30 children assembled carrying placards reading 'We Want Our Parents', 'Why Must They Starve?' and 'I Want My Mummy!' As a crowd of spectators gathered and foreign television crews arrived, a deputation including Ilse Fischer, Toni Bernstein and Mark Weinberg went inside the City

Hall to ask the mayor's help in obtaining the release of their parents. While they were there, the police turned up, arrested the children and took them off to the police station at Marshall Square. When Ilse and her two friends discovered what had happened, they raced over to Marshall Square and demanded that they too should be arrested. Ilse phoned Bram to tell him the news. 'I said, "Look, I'm sorry but we're all in Marshall Square. Can you come and get us?"' Ilse recalled. 'And Bram came and signed receipts for all the kids and we were all released. And he said to me afterwards, "You know, you shouldn't have phoned me. You should have let them sort out what they were going to do with you." Which was quite a tough line to take because they were little kids and we'd been there for a couple of hours.'

The following day, a party was held at Beaumont Street with cakes and ice-creams for the children. Press photographers were on hand to record the event. In Cape Town Ruth played her part by leading a children's delegation to parliament with a petition addressed to the minister of justice.

But by then the women detainees had decided to call off their hunger strike. Doctors had warned that three of them would harm themselves irreparably if they continued. Nevertheless, they had gained national attention.

The Afrikaans press, noting the role played by the two Fischer daughters in leading demonstrations in Johannesburg and Cape Town, remarked on how far such a distinguished Afrikaner family had fallen into bad ways. Writing in the Cape nationalist paper, *Die Burger*, the columnist 'Dawie' recalled family history starting with Abraham Fischer and went on to comment about the promise Bram had once seemed to offer. In his youth, said Dawie, he had been bright, conscientious, cultivated and lovable. But in Johannesburg he had become 'more and more left – and that goes for his wife as well'. A wide chasm had developed between the political attitude of Abraham Fischer and his grandson. *'Die appel het ver van die boom geval'* – 'The apple has fallen far from the tree.'

As one of the few senior figures in the Communist Party left untouched by the state of emergency, Bram was actively engaged from the start in trying to rebuild its underground structure. New cells and new committees had to be established; new recruits were needed.

Bram acted as a key link between the small leadership group which had evaded arrest – Michael Harmel, Moses Kotane and Ben Turok – and the outside world. Much depended on party supporters not known to the Special Branch – members of C group, as they were called – who were able to provide safe houses and act as couriers without attracting undue attention. 'First of all we had to get together the people who were still around,' recalled Esther Barsel, a party member since the 1940s who became a key figure in C-group activities. 'We had to make contact with them. Those who were not in groups, those who were around singly, had to be contacted singly.'

Other key figures in C group included Ralph and Mini Sepel whom Bram recruited during the state of emergency. Mini became an underground librarian, collecting communist literature mailed from England and redistributing it to various addresses in Johannesburg. Their house in Observatory became a regular meeting place and hideout for members not only of the Communist Party but of the banned African National Congress. The Sepels were careful to avoid contact with other activists, and their involvement remained undetected for several years.

As well as recruits to the Communist Party, there was an influx of young dissident whites into the ranks of the Congress of Democrats and other anti-apartheid organisations, prompted by the massacre at Sharpeville and the government's use of emergency laws, mass arrests and banning orders. They came from a new generation of whites alarmed by the onset of totalitarian rule and determined to make their protest clear.

But far more radical ideas were being considered within the communist hierarchy. From his hideout in Johannesburg, moving between ten different houses in five months, Michael Harmel produced a paper arguing that it was necessary to abandon non-violence as the sole means of struggle and move to armed methods. Harmel led a disorganised life. He was a moody, irritable personality, with few social graces, known to be unkind to his wife. But he was highly regarded as the party's leading theoretician, admired for his analytical mind, and a major influence on his colleagues, including Bram. Ben Turok, who spent five months with him during the state of emergency, described him as 'the Lenin of the movement'. Harmel's view was adamant: 'No further progress is possible along the traditional paths or by adhering strictly to the non-violence slogan in a situation where every democratic demand or criticism is treated as an act of rebellion or treason.' Such was the respect in which Harmel was held that the idea of armed action gained immediate credibility.

Among the detainees in prison, similar thoughts were brewing, not just among communists but among other radicals. In the wake of the Sharpeville crisis, many activists came to believe that the use of violence offered the only way forward. In Pretoria, an odd assortment of radicals gathered around Monty Berman, a communist recently expelled from the party who harboured romantic notions of leading his own guerrilla army.

The need for action of some kind was seen as paramount. In June Bram, now acting chairman of the Communist Party, presided over a clandestine meeting held in a brickfield near Kempton Park, east of Johannesburg, at which delegates voted in favour of the party coming out into the open and raising its own standard. In July, after seven years of secret underground activity undetected by the Special Branch, the Communist Party distributed leaflets announcing its existence and called on workers to rally in the struggle against the government.

As the emergency continued, twice a week Bram drove to Pretoria to visit Molly in prison where she was slowly recovering from the hunger strike. 'I'm not as bonny as I used to be,' she had confessed to Bram during its final stages. Then on 1 July she was released, along with 1 200 other detainees. Setting off late from Johannesburg, Bram, Ruth and Ilse arrived in Pretoria to find Molly sitting on her suitcase outside the prison gate wondering why no one had come to collect her.

As a result of the government's decision to relax the emergency regulations, the defence lawyers in the treason trial returned to court at the end of July. Bram was given the task of handling the most damaging piece of evidence produced by the prosecution: a tape recording, made by a Special Branch detective hiding in a room adjacent to the ANC's headquarters, of a speech by the ANC's Sophia-town leader, Robert Resha. Addressing a group of volunteers, Resha had emphasised the need for discipline by saying: 'When you are disciplined and you are told by the organisation not to be violent, you

op: Three generations of Fischer's: Bram's ther Percy *(left)*, his son Paul and Bram the 1950s. *(UWC/Robben Island Museum)*

Bottom: Bram Fischer with his children. *(From left)* Ruth, Bram, Ilse and Paul. *(Sunday Times)*

Right and below:
Molly Krige came
from an Afrikaner
family with a
lineage as
distinguished as
that of the Fischers.
Pictured here in her
early thirties *(Family
archives)* and in later
years, she was the
love of Bram's life
and also formed a
remarkable
partnership with
him. Bram never
properly recovered
from her death in a
car accident.
*(UWC/Robben Island
Museum)*

p: The Fischer's house at No 12 Beaumont
eet, Oaklands, Johannesburg. It became an
sis for friends and acquaintances of all races
ermined to keep alive the idea of a
ltiracial world and also a centre of intrigue.
mily archives)

Bottom: Communist comrades: Ruth First,
Bram Fischer *(standing)*, Joe Slovo and Rusty
Bernstein on the podium at a Communist
Party meeting in the late 1940s.
(UWC/Robben Island Museum)

Right: Nelson Mandela said of Fischer: 'Bram's commitment to the struggle helped to change many of us in the ANC from being Africanists to believers in non-racial democracy.'
(UWC/Robben Island Museum)

Below: Lilliesleaf Farm, the underground Communist Party headquarters in Rivonia, Sandton, which Nelson Mandela and other ANC conspirators used when launching armed rebellion against the government.
(Sunday Times)

Dear Kim,

88,76,73,166: I have now ascertained that the losses caused by this accident may be more farreaching than I anticipated. Ofcourse I do not doubt his constitutional strength and I remain sure that he will recover. What is disturbing, however, is that on the evening before the accident he was handed your latest balance sheet (22,85,83,81,98) for transmission to me. This, in ordinary circumstances would not be serious, but two things are of importance. If there was anything arising from your statement that I should act on urgently, then you must send me a duplicate immediately — do so in any case, as I shall not be able to find out for some time where he left it if it was not on his person.

The other thing is that he may, as was sometimes his custom, have scribbled his personal comments on the documents. These as you will realise, may have been of a highly confidential character, and if, for instance, they were to be examined by the police or some insurance assessor, we might receive much adverse publicity.

With regard to the former, I shall append hereto a 72,135,78,98,92, just in case anything has gone wrong in that direction

With regard to the latter I suggest we immediately 88,67,83,28, 84,81,82,56,85,66,75,69,68,61,52,86,47,44 airmail. 15,65,57,70,2,24. means 21,50,161,60,33,39,78,28,54,22 broken up for safety's sake by a 92,32,71,24,151, which must ofcourse, in calculations, be ignored.

77,52,5,146,26: This company was called upon earlier this week to produce 18,10,55,63,29,39,30,6529,47,21,41,37,43,12,45,1,36,71,28, 51,5. It flatly refused to do so: 11,29,57,19,13,3,31,75 . This ofcourse has all been hushed up. I wonder if there is anything you can do about it. 46,65,48,22,6,27,56,30,26 commented on this.

142,73,40,52: The last three copies have arrived, two went to 88,54, 67 and one to 46,8. You are therefore entitled to 98,49,36,80,49; 1,74,78,6,2,22,6,17,64,34,50;52,70,66,85,39,16,41;142,77,10,34,21, 140,92. As I told you this firm is not authorised, nor apparently willing to print any further copies. For the moment you must assume that this is final unless fresh authority is issued from your end and it is found to be physically possible here. This is why I urge you to deal immediately with15,18,23,27,64; 6,34,88,60 as I have already suggested, or with some other reputable firm with whom I or 22,85,5, can work. I assume that you

...art of an encoded letter which Bram ...ischer wrote just before his arrest on ...1 November 1965. Found at an address in ...orlett Drive, Johannesburg. (Sunday Times)

Gerard Ludi, the police spy who succeeded in penetrating the underground Communist Party cell which Bram Fischer attended.
(Sunday Times)

Joel Joffee, one of the defence lawyers in the Rivonia Trial. He said of Bram: 'He had a charm, a great gentleness and a personal sincerity which endeared him to everybody.'
(Sunday Times)

Sitting on a park bench while out on bail before going underground, Bram Fischer appeared the embodiment of respectability, but led a complex double life.
(Sunday Times)

Bram Fischer in disguise: His thick grey hair was shaved back to give him a receding hairline and he grew a goatee beard, which made him resemble Lenin.
(UWC/Robben Island Museum)

No. 29.

TRANSVAAL PROVINCE
Road Traffic Ordinance, 1957
DRIVER'S LICENCE
Section 65 (3)

PROVINSIE TRANSVAAL
Padverkeersordonnansie, 1957
DRYWERSLISENSIE
Artikel 65 (3)

NO. 887

Surname: MR. BLACK .... Familienaam.

Christian names: DOUGLAS .... Voorname.

Address: 63 CARLTON, ELOFF STREET, ... Adres.
.... J O H A N N E S B U R G.

Race: EUROPEAN .... Ras.

Identity No.: .... Persoonsnommer.
(where applicable/waar van toepassing)

is hereby licensed to drive the following class of motor vehicle as contemplated in Section 58 of the Ordinance, without/with glasses:

word hierby gelisensieer om die volgende klas motorvoertuig, soos beoog in Artikel 58 van die Ordonnansie, te dryf sonder/met bril.:

LIGHT MOTOR VEHICLE

Essential modifications of vehicle: NIL — NUL   Noodsaaklike wysigings van voertuig:

No. and date of certificate of competence: 785   9.2.59   No. en datum van bevoegdheidsertifikaat:

Amount paid receipt of which is hereby acknowledged: See cash register imprint.

Bedrag betaal: ontvangs waarvan hierby erken word.— Sien kasregistersyfers.

Signature of licensee .... Handtekening van lisensiehouer.

ENDORSEMENTS / ENDOSSEMENTE.

For Registering Authority — Namens registrasie-owerheid van
JOHANNESBURG.

80/1550 Dyneco, 2911/11/58

Bram Fischer used an English name, Douglas Black, as his main alias during his life underground. This is the forged driver's licence he used at that time.
(Sunday Times)

Part of the
equipment that
Bram Fischer used
for his disguises
underground: make-
up, false moustache
and tweezers. It was
used as police
evidence at the trial.
(Sunday Times/
George Els)

Above left: Percy Yutar, prosecutor in the Rivonia Trial, who argued for the death sentence for Mandela and the other conspirators. *(Sunday Times)*

Above right: Walter Sisulu, Nelson Mandela's mentor, often visited the Fischers at their home in Beaumont Street. 'A perfect gentleman,' said Sisulu. 'His manner made it difficult for people to say no.' *(Sunday Times)*

Below: Arthur Goldreich *(left)* and Harold Wolpe, two leading Rivonia conspirators, whose escape Bram Fischer helped to organise. *(Sunday Times)*

Left: Ruth First, whose ordeal in solitary confinement led her to attempt suicide, eventually accepted the government's offer of a one-way exit permit. With her children Gillian and Robyn.
(Sunday Times)

Below: Ivan Schermbrucker, one of Bram Fischer's closest friends, who was tortured and imprisoned. His wife Lesley, one of Bram's main contacts after he went underground, was also subsequently imprisoned.
(Sunday Times/ Rodney Celliers)

Above left: Joe
Slovo, a fervent
advocate of
revolutionary
warfare, one of the
authors of
Operation
Mayibuye.
(Sunday Times)

Above right: Mary
Benson, the South
African writer
based in London,
visited Bram in
1964 while he was
underground. 'It's
like the coming of a
whole battalion,'
Bram said of her.
(Sunday Times)

Below: Rusty and
Hilda Bernstein
with their daughter
Toni and son-in-law
Ivan Strasburg
leaving court.
(Sunday Times)

must not be violent. If you are a true volunteer and you are called upon to be violent, you must be absolutely violent, you must murder, murder! That is all.' According to the prosecution, this was clear evidence of the violent purpose of the ANC.

Bram began by taking Resha calmly though the circumstances of the destruction of Sophiatown, a multiracial enclave in Johannesburg surrounded by white suburbs, which the government had been determined to excise from the map, while the ANC had mounted a campaign of resistance. He then questioned Resha on the nature of ANC policy, about its attitude to violence. Resha replied that the ANC pursued a policy of non-violence, a policy with which he agreed. How then could he reconcile his speech with ANC policy? asked Bram. 'The example I used in that speech cannot be reconciled with the policy of the African National Congress,' replied Resha simply.

The state of emergency was lifted on 31 August, enabling the defendants in the treason trial to go home for the first time in five months and the trial itself to proceed in easier circumstances. Beaumont Street once again became a hive of activity. A young Afrikaner teacher, Marius Schoon, remembered how in those months a group of young white and Indian activists would gather there on most Saturday and Sunday afternoons, enjoying the Fischers' warm hospitality and lively intellectual discussions about South Africa's future. 'It was the most important period of their lives,' he said. Visitors dropped by at all hours of the day and night, and were rarely turned away. Marius Schoon recalled a convivial late-night party which was interrupted by Bram calling down from his bedroom window only to ask for a little less noise as he had to deal with a major case in the courts next morning.

With the release of many of its activists, the Communist Party began functioning with new vigour. Molly joined a group of four which included two close friends: Hilda Bernstein, a party member since the 1930s who had led the hunger strike in prison, and Violet Weinberg, a formidable Jewish lady and long-time party member who had also participated in the hunger strike. The fourth member of the group was a young recruit, Jean Middleton, a Durban-born teacher who had joined the Congress of Democrats before moving to Johannesburg.

In the inner circle there was intense discussion about the use of violence. Michael Harmel was adamant that the apartheid regime was bound to collapse. It was, he said, 'a kind of freak, an anachronism which cannot hope much longer to survive'. Violence would hasten its end. A group of revolutionary enthusiasts, seeing themselves in the tradition of Marxist-Leninist revolutionaries determined to strike against a brutal, decaying regime, longed for action. At the forefront of this group was Joe Slovo, a hard-line Stalinist with romantic notions about revolutionary warfare, recently released from prison.

There were also voices of caution. The party's secretary-general, Moses Kotane, a Moscow-trained party worker renowned for his hard-headed realism, was worried that violence would undermine the ability of an underground movement to continue with non-violent political work. The potential for conventional political struggle, he argued, had by no means been exhausted.

Bram also had his doubts as to whether an underground movement could mount a campaign of violence as well as survive the repression that would inevitably follow. He was anxious about taking steps from which there could be no retreat. But ultimately he became a reluctant convert to the idea of armed struggle, conceding that every other alternative had been tried, to no avail.

At a secret meeting in December 1960 at a private house in Victoria, a white suburb in Johannesburg, the communists took the decision to establish an armed force consisting of small squads of saboteurs as a prelude to engaging in guerrilla warfare.

The treason trial, meanwhile, four years after it had started, lumbered into its concluding stages. The prosecution's closing argument, begun on 7 November 1960, ended, after several adjournments, on 6 March 1961. Maisels then opened the defence's closing arguments by refuting all charges of violence. 'We admit that there is a question of non-cooperation and passive resistance,' he said. 'We shall say quite frankly that if non-cooperation and passive resistance constitute high treason, then we are guilty. But these are plainly not encompassed in the law of treason.'

So complex were many of the issues involved that the defence team had expected their closing arguments to take up to three months to present. Bram, who had been given the massive task of analysing the

ANC's policies, had spent weeks in careful preparation. But no sooner was he in his stride than the judges made a series of interruptions directing him to focus on specific issues. Finally, on 23 March, in a further dramatic intervention, they adjourned for six days to consider whether they could forgo hearing certain aspects of the defence argument, in the interests of shortening the trial. The clear implication was that they had already made up their minds in favour of acquittal.

After watching the drama unfold from the spectators' gallery, Molly wrote to Bram:

> I was so proud of you today, you looked so distinguished with your long-cut greying hair, wearing your sober black. Now don't let the word 'sober' set you off imagining that I'm the very opposite. I admit that I have been terribly excited all evening since you phoned to say that rumour had it that it won't be long now ...
>
> Darling, the accused say you were wonderful; Leon [Levy] said that he was listening carefully for the 1st time in 4 yrs ... Someone else said that from the time you took over, kindliness descended over the whole court!
>
> I'm not underestimating the role played by the rest of your team, but I'm certain you've been the key pin and if we win, well ...?

On 29 March Judge Rumpff delivered the court's findings. It was clear, he said, that the ANC and its allies had been working 'to replace the present form of state with a radically and fundamentally different form of state'. But although there had been some violent speeches by ANC members, there was no proof of an ANC policy of violent revolution. Nor was there any proof that the ANC was a communist organisation or that it had been infiltrated by communists, or that the Freedom Charter envisaged a communist state. The cornerstone of the case, he said, was the ANC's policy of incitement to violence. The prosecution's failure to prove this policy inevitably meant the collapse of its case. Accordingly, he found the accused not guilty and discharged them.

Outside the court, as the accused celebrated their release amid a throng of friends and family, laughing, weeping and crying, Maisels and Bram were hoisted high above their shoulders. 'Some of the congratulations have been most touching,' Bram wrote to his daughters in Cape Town. 'Apart from the cables from overseas, what is most heart-warming is the Africans who stop me in the corridor or in the street or in the Court – men I don't seem to know at all who shake me by the hand and say thank you.'

That night, Bram gave a huge party at Beaumont Street for the accused. As guests arrived, Special Branch detectives watched from two cars parked in the street outside.

CHAPTER 6

SPEAR OF THE NATION

Bram's life from 1961 became increasingly complex. Ostensibly, he remained a pillar of respectability. In 1961 he was elected chairman of the Bar Council. His talents as a lawyer capable of mastering the most abstruse legal and financial cases were still sought by large corporations. In secret, he was the head of a revolutionary communist movement and a leading conspirator in a plot to launch armed rebellion against the government.

By mid-1961 the communists were well advanced in their preparations for armed struggle. A channel for funds from Moscow and other foreign sources had been set up through a travel agency in Loveday Street. Small specialist units for sabotage activity had begun trying their hand at cutting telephone and communications links. Plans were under way to send recruits to China for military training.

In July, the party acquired a smallholding of 28 acres called Lilliesleaf Farm in a secluded, wooded hollow in the Rivonia area, about ten miles north of Johannesburg, for use as its underground headquarters. The main house there, set well back from the dirt road which passed the farm, was spacious, with whitewashed walls, large curved windows at the front and a high shingle roof, a desirable residence for a wealthy family. Behind it stood a large, imposing thatch-roofed cottage and an assortment of outbuildings, storerooms, fuel sheds, workrooms and servants' quarters. The plan was for Lilliesleaf to be used, by all outward appearances, as a normal white smallholding, and for the main house to be occupied by a party member, Arthur Goldreich, and his family.

Michael Harmel, adopting a false name, handled the transaction with an estate agent; Harold Wolpe, a communist lawyer, helped set up a dummy company to buy the property; and Vivian Ezra, a party member unknown to the Special Branch, was made the nominal owner.

Bram, as well as heading the central committee, was involved in keeping track of party funds. He held regular meetings with the party treasurer, Julius First, Ruth First's father, a retired businessman who, according to his granddaughter, Gillian Slovo, had 'the soul of an accountant and the convictions of a revolutionary'. First operated from the offices of a Johannesburg publishing company which was used to launder party funds.

The publishing company was owned by Mannie Brown, another businessman with a taste for revolutionary politics. During the state of emergency, Mannie had spent several months in detention in the company of Joe Slovo, an old friend. 'Very much like my father-in-law Julius,' Slovo recalled, 'Mannie combined an extraordinary private and social generosity with a hard-headed approach towards the "dog-eat-dog" ethic of so-called free enterprise.' An inveterate poker player, he used bridge and poker games at his house in Orchards as a cover for clandestine activity. Bram often went there, but never played.

The momentum toward violence gathered pace. In June, shortly after the government had suppressed a national protest campaign with a massive display of military and police strength, leaders of the banned African National Congress met in secret to decide whether to embark on armed struggle. Nelson Mandela, who had been operating from underground since the end of the treason trial, argued vigorously that there was no realistic alternative. Violence, he said, had become inevitable, whether or not it was initiated by the ANC. ANC supporters were beginning to lose confidence in the policy of non-violence and would eventually resort to violent methods of protest of their own. It would be far better for the ANC to channel and control the impetus toward violence to ensure it was directed at proper targets. A campaign of sabotage would scare off foreign investors, disrupt trade and cause sufficient damage to the economy to force the government to change course.

Mandela's views were influenced both by the communists' enthusiasm for armed struggle and by the heady examples of revolutionary activity elsewhere in the world. By mid-1961, Algerian nationalists were on the verge of victory over French forces seeking to defend the white settler population. In Cuba, Fidel Castro's revolution showed how a small group of revolutionaries could gain mass support to win power. What made a particular impact from the Cuban example was Che Guevara's 'detonator' theory, the idea that armed action on its own would create a momentum among the population. Revolutionary enthusiasts like Joe Slovo argued that sabotage would provide a bridge to popular armed struggle, drawing in new recruits and conditioning the population to accept methods of violence, eventually leading to a broad revolutionary assault on the government.

A major obstacle, however, was the position of Chief Luthuli, the ANC president, a man of great moral authority with an unshakeable commitment to non-violence. Luthuli was convinced that non-violence was the only justifiable course of action on both moral and practical grounds. He placed great faith in the moral impact on whites of the African struggle for political rights, and possessed an abiding optimism that whites would sooner or later be compelled to change heart.

After hours of argument, however, he agreed to a compromise. The ANC would remain committed to non-violence, but it would not stand in the way of members who wanted to establish a separate and independent military organisation.

The new organisation, Umkhonto we Sizwe, or Spear of the Nation, was essentially a joint venture between the ANC and the Communist Party. Mandela was chosen as chairman and Slovo as chief-of-staff. Neither of them had any experience of sabotage or guerrilla warfare. Mandela knew literally nothing in practice about what was involved. Slovo's experience had been limited to his role in a signals unit in the closing stages of the Second World War in Italy; he had never taken part in combat. Few others were any more knowledgeable. Umkhonto's first instructor was Jack Hodgson, a 'desert rat' who had served in a tank corps in North Africa and who also had knowledge of explosives gained while working in the mines. A resourceful man, he turned his own flat, on the fourth floor of a block in Hillbrow, into a bomb laboratory and later into a bomb factory. But from the start there was a large degree of amateurism about Umkhonto.

The strategy decided upon by the Umkhonto high command was twofold. First, a sabotage campaign would be carried out against targets like government buildings and installations, railways, power plants and telecommunications; second, preparations would be made for guerrilla warfare if the sabotage campaign failed to get the government to change its policies.

As well as serving as headquarters for the Communist Party, Lilliesleaf now became the main base for Umkhonto. Frequent meetings were held there, with visitors coming and going at all hours. Nelson Mandela, on the run from the police, took up residence in the thatched cottage, staying there during the day, leaving for assignments at night, and spending weekends there with his wife Winnie and their children. There were soon problems over security.

Bram, given charge of a security committee, was infuriated by security lapses. 'He had a huge temper when somebody broke security,' recalled Bob Hepple, a young lawyer whom Bram had recruited to the Communist Party. 'He would go red in the face and really scream at a person. There was a total explosion when something went wrong.' He was particularly exasperated by Michael Harmel, who was invariably sloppy about underground work. Mandela recalled returning to Lilliesleaf late one night to find the house lights on, the front door open, the radio at full blast and Harmel fast asleep in bed. When Mandela woke him up, he complained: 'Nel, must you disturb my sleep? Can't this wait until tomorrow?'

The date set for the start of the sabotage campaign was 16 December 1961, a day then known as the Day of the Covenant, on which whites celebrated their victory over the Zulu chief Dingaan at the Battle of Blood River in 1838. Bombs exploded that night at government buildings in Johannesburg, Durban and Port Elizabeth. Leaflets left behind on the streets announced the formation of Umkhonto with the warning: 'The time comes in the life of any nation when there remain only two choices: submit or fight. That time has now come.' The leaflets added: 'We hope, even at this late hour, that our first actions will awaken everyone to a realisation of the disastrous situation to which the Nationalist policy is leading. We hope that we will bring the government and its supporters to their senses before it is too late, so that both the government and its policies can be changed before matters reach the desperate stage of civil war.'

Over the course of the next 18 months, sabotage attacks continued sporadically, mainly on public buildings, railway lines and power installations. Most of the attacks were clumsy and ineffectual, none causing any lasting damage. One white activist was arrested in Port Elizabeth after he had tested his home-made bombs by setting them off in his back yard on a quiet Sunday afternoon.

Sabotage attacks were also carried out by another group, the National Committee for Liberation, consisting mainly of young white left-wing intellectuals led by Monty Berman, but with little result. One of Berman's early efforts was described by Hugh Lewin, a young journalist whom he recruited and who later was to befriend Bram: 'They went out with a hacksaw, and they went to a place in the Magaliesberg where they'd found a pylon on a hill, and they spent several weekends returning to this place with a hacksaw and sawing through this thing which never fell.' In later attempts, the National Committee of Liberation managed to dismantle power lines and disrupt telephone services. 'I thought that sabotage might shock the whites into awareness of the conditions under which the blacks were living and, in due time, change the system,' said Lewin.

As well as sabotage activities, Umkhonto laid plans for embarking on guerrilla warfare. Recruits were sent for training in China under an arrangement already set up by the Communist Party. In January 1962, Mandela left South Africa surreptitiously, crossing the border into Bechuanaland, to seek support from independent African states. He himself underwent a brief course of military training in Ethiopia. But less than two weeks after his return to South Africa in July, careless about his own personal security, he was captured by police while travelling between Durban and Johannesburg. Whatever suspicions the police may have had, however, they possessed no evidence to link Mandela with Umkhonto and the sabotage campaign. In court, he was charged with no more than inciting African workers to strike and leaving the country without valid travel documents, and sentenced to five years' imprisonment.

The government reacted to the sabotage campaign, not by instituting reforms, as Mandela had hoped, but by imposing increasingly ruthless counter-measures. Prime Minister Hendrik Verwoerd appointed a new minister of justice, John Vorster, a former Nazi sympathiser who had been imprisoned without trial during the Second World War for pro-German activities. Verwoerd gave him instructions to root out all resistance. A new head of the security police, Hendrik van den Bergh, also a former Nazi sympathiser, was installed. At 'the Grays', the headquarters of the security police on Von Wielligh Street, a new breed of police interrogator moved in, ready to use any method necessary to obtain information.

Vorster quickly put into operation new laws which gave him virtually unlimited power. Under the *General Law Amendment Act* of 1962, or the *'Sabotage' Act* as it was generally known, Vorster was empowered to order the 'house arrest' of anyone he considered a threat to security. He could prohibit persons banned or listed under the *Suppression of Communism Act* from preparing anything for publication, from communicating with one another, from having visitors, from joining organisations, from attending social gatherings. Nothing written or spoken by banned persons was allowed to be published or reproduced in South Africa.

In 1962 Vorster silenced 102 people under the 'gagging' clause of the Act, including Bram and Molly. He also listed 437 people as communists, placed 18 people under house arrest, outlawed the Congress of Democrats, banned the radical weekly newspaper *New Age*, and prohibited protest meetings on the steps of the Johannesburg City Hall.

The communist network began to crumble. Jack Hodgson, the bomb-maker, was placed under 24-hour house arrest in his Hillbrow flat for five years, and his wife, Rica, under 12-hour house arrest. As both were banned persons, they needed special ministerial dispensation to communicate with each other. The Hodgsons eventually fled the country. Michael Harmel and Moses Kotane were placed under 24-hour house arrest. They too made plans to leave. Rusty Bernstein, placed under dusk-to-dawn house arrest, resolved to stay, but found it increasingly hard to find work as an architect.

Bram was adamantly opposed to anyone leaving, and did his best to calm the fears of those worried about the dangers of staying. Among them was AnnMarie Wolpe, the wife of the communist lawyer, Harold Wolpe, who was expecting their third child. 'During my pregnancy I constantly raised the possibility of our leaving the country, even though Harold's whole life was so wrapped up in the liberation movement,' she recalled in her account of these events. 'I was frightened of moving. I was frightened of staying. No longer did I feel smug about sticking it out in South Africa. I had become more and more pessimistic, convinced that it was only a matter of time before Harold landed up in jail. His continued political activity no longer seemed worthwhile.'

Eventually Harold Wolpe agreed that she should have a talk to Bram – 'a man of unimpeachable integrity and gentleness', she wrote, 'a man who commanded respect and love from all'. They arranged to meet at a weekend retreat overlooking the Hartbeespoortdam owned by her brother, Jimmy Kantor, a criminal lawyer with no political connections who was also Wolpe's partner.

'Bram listened sympathetically to all my fears about Harold's safety,' she wrote. 'I did not raise my needs or anxieties. After all, I was the non-active wife who was not at risk. Although he did not minimise the stress and strain of the type of life we were leading, Bram painted a realistic picture of what people like himself and Harold were likely to face in the future. "I don't for one moment underestimate the difficulties we all face, yet it is crucial that people like Harold continue with their work." It was not just his work in the courts defending political cases, said Bram. "He is playing an extremely significant role in the struggle – the more so as there are relatively few whites prepared to join with the blacks in the struggle." Bram emphasised this last point. It made me proud of what Harold was doing. He convinced us that we should not contemplate moving yet. "If the time comes for Harold to leave, the movement would provide every assistance, as it has done with other people," he reassured me.' Harold Wolpe remembered: 'Bram helped us clear our minds, and we stayed on.'

Bram was also conscientious about keeping up the spirits of activists already in difficulty. When Kathy Kathrada, a leading Indian conspirator under dusk-to-dawn house arrest, answered the door bell on his birthday, he found a bottle of brandy on the doorstep and caught a glimpse of Bram disappearing round the corner.

Despite the difficulties, the Communist Party held a national conference in Greenside, a Johannesburg suburb, in November 1962. Delegates formally adopted a policy document entitled 'The Road to South African Freedom' setting out the party's two-stage theory on revolution. Bram had had a hand in drafting it but was not present at

67

the conference. In the first stage, the party envisaged 'a united front of national liberation' consisting of a Communist Party alliance with the ANC through the military wing of Umkhonto, which would set out 'to destroy white domination'. In the second stage, South Africa would be transformed into a socialist state.

For a group of revolutionary enthusiasts, however, the revolution in the field was already moving too slowly. Far from being daunted by the government's increasing use of repression, they believed that the phase of limited sabotage had effectively run its course and that the only remaining option was to commit Umkhonto to revolutionary violence. At the forefront of this group was Joe Slovo. Together with another Communist Party veteran, Govan Mbeki, he drew up a strategy for guerrilla warfare on a scale that no one had previously contemplated. Their plan, named Operation Mayibuye, envisaged the recruitment of an army of some 7 000 guerrillas across the country who would link up with armed groups returning by sea and by air from training abroad. They also proposed the large-scale manufacture of hand grenades, bombs and other armaments inside South Africa. 'The time for small thinking is over,' they declared.

The contents of Operation Mayibuye were debated at length again and again at Lilliesleaf. The revolutionary enthusiasts wanted its immediate adoption. But many others were deeply sceptical. Bram thought it 'an entirely unrealistic brainchild of some youthful and adventurous imagination'.

Nevertheless, parts of the plan were set in motion. A new property near Krugersdorp named Travallyn was purchased for use as an arsenal. 'Production requirements' were estimated at 48 000 land mines, 210 000 hand grenades and 1 500 time devices for bombs. A 30-year-old engineer, Denis Goldberg, who came from a well-known communist family, was given responsibility for arms manufacture at Travallyn and opened negotiations for production equipment from factory owners, wholesale distributors and machinery merchants using a string of pseudonyms. Arthur Goldreich, who had previously travelled to China, the Soviet Union and East Germany seeking military aid for Umkhonto and obtaining information on the manufacture of arms, produced a design for a hand grenade. Julius First, the treasurer, was instructed to acquire a ship for ferrying recruits out of the country.

Slovo himself left South Africa in June 1963 to canvass for support from foreign governments for Operation Mayibuye.

At Lilliesleaf, the comings and goings of the conspirators were so frequent that it resembled more a business enterprise than the secret headquarters of a revolutionary movement. Bram was a regular visitor. Slovo, before his departure, went there, driving from his office in Innes Chambers in town, as many as three times a day. As well as Arthur Goldreich and his family who lived there as residents, the farm buildings were used for meetings of the party's central committee and Umkhonto's high command. Goldberg often drove across from Travallyn. Bernstein, despite his banning order, frequently turned up. Conspirators on the run, like Walter Sisulu and Govan Mbeki, spent long spells there. A variety of Umkhonto personnel passed through. The number of people who knew of its location was becoming dangerously large. The conspirators often talked of moving their meetings elsewhere, but still they kept coming back.

Yet the risks were becoming manifestly greater by the day. In May 1963, Vorster introduced new emergency laws empowering the police to arrest without warrant and detain any person suspected of having committed sabotage or any offences under the *Suppression of Communism Act*, or any person suspected of possessing information about such offences. Detainees could be held in solitary confinement without access to lawyers and family until they had replied 'satisfactorily' to all questions put by police interrogators. The initial period for which they could be held was 90 days. But the police were entitled to renew the order again and again – 'until this side of eternity', according to Vorster. The Act expressly prohibited the courts from ordering the release of a detainee. Scores of men and women now vanished into jail, to be subjected to solitary confinement and prolonged interrogation.

With information obtained from detainees and informers, the security police soon identified Lilliesleaf as a suspect location. Raiding the farm on 11 July 1963 they caught a whole collection of leading conspirators who had gathered there, including Sisulu, Mbeki, Goldberg, Goldreich, Bernstein, Kathrada and the lawyer Bob Hepple. They also acquired a massive haul of documents relating to revolutionary methods, arms production, guerrilla recruitment and training, contacts with

China, the Soviet Union and East European governments, evidence about the involvement of Nelson Mandela, maps pinpointing targets for attack, and the plan for guerrilla warfare, Operation Mayibuye. Some of the documents implicated Bram.

CHAPTER 7

THE FALLOUT

News of the arrests at Lilliesleaf, carried by the Johannesburg news-paper *Die Transvaler*, threw the conspirators still at large into turmoil. Bram and Molly frantically tried to contact those activists most at risk. Molly dashed round to warn Harold Wolpe. As the lawyer who had handled the Lilliesleaf transaction, he was particularly vulnerable. He had also just completed drafting a disciplinary code for Umkhonto, and his handwriting and fingerprints were on that and other documents likely to have been seized at Lilliesleaf. Molly appeared at his house looking drawn and haggard. 'Oh, Harold, it's a calamity,' she said. 'They got them all at Rivonia yesterday.' Wolpe was aghast. 'My God, Molly, what the hell are we going to do?' As he walked Molly back to her car, they could find nothing to say, not even goodbye.

Wolpe knew that it was only a matter of hours before the police came for him. In rising panic and despair, he fled to a cottage over-looking Hartbeespoortdam in the Magaliesberg hills, after telling Bram where he was going. The next morning Bram arrived with Ivan Schermbrucker, a long-time Communist Party member and one of his closest friends. He told Wolpe that he would have to leave the country immediately but that he could offer no assistance. 'We've taken a helluva beating,' he said. 'You're on your own. We just have no resources available to help you at the moment.'

Wolpe had no passport, no ready cash, nor could he think of a viable plan. He travelled back to Johannesburg to hide in a friend's flat in Hillbrow, then drove to a farm near Rustenburg where his wife, AnnMarie, and their children were staying with relatives.

'Nobody can help me,' he told her. 'It's up to me to arrange my escape.' AnnMarie was flabbergasted. 'But they said they had an escape route all worked out. I was convinced of that. Bram told me not to worry. I believed him.' Wolpe replied that the arrests had been catastrophic. 'Nobody is able to help me at all,' he said. 'I've been told that I've got to make my own way. Every man for himself.'

With the help of some friends, he tried to cross the border into Bechuanaland but ran straight into a border police patrol. He was arrested, driven back to Johannesburg and held in Marshall Square police station in Johannesburg in the same cell as Goldreich.

Other conspirators were also in immediate danger. Like Harold Wolpe, Vivian Ezra had been involved in the Lilliesleaf transaction. But what especially alarmed Bram was that, during the state of emergency, Ezra, a secret communist unknown to the Special Branch, had been given the task of memorising the names and addresses of other secret communists – D group, as they were known – so that they could be contacted if necessary. Ezra's arrest therefore could have brought disastrous consequences.

Fearing the worst, Bram raced round to seek the help of David Kitson, an Umkhonto instructor who had been due to attend the fatal Lilliesleaf meeting but who fortuitously had been confined to bed with influenza that day. Bram explained that it was imperative to get Ezra out of the country as fast as possible. Together they organised an escape committee, bringing in Hilda Bernstein, Ivan Schermbrucker and Mannie Brown. Using the good offices of a churchman whom Bram knew, the committee devised an escape route to a mission station across the border in Swaziland. Within days, Ezra was spirited out of the country.

The escape committee next became involved in trying to spring Wolpe and Goldreich from prison, using Wolpe's wife, AnnMarie, who was allowed to visit him, as an intermediary. Bram was at first sceptical about the plan, pointing out that it would take all their remaining resources just to hide the men. Most supporters were lying low, fearful of the consequences of further involvement. When Bram drew up a list of supporters who might provide a refuge, 11 of the 12 approached refused to help.

Meanwhile, inside Marshall Square, Wolpe and Goldreich, after trying unsuccessfully to saw their way through prison bars with blades smuggled in by AnnMarie, managed to secure the co-operation of a young Afrikaner warder by offering him a large bribe. Two Indian activists held in the same cell block joined the plot. Bram purchased an escape car and arranged for a driver to pick up the prisoners at night in a street adjacent to the police station. For two nights, the driver waited in vain for them to arrive.

On the third night, after a frustrating delay caused by a sudden change in prison routine, the four men escaped through the prison gates only to find that their getaway driver had already left. The two Indians made off on foot in one direction, Wolpe and Goldreich in another, heading for the flat in Hillbrow that Wolpe had recently used. No one was there. In increasing desperation, they decided to try the only other possible refuge they knew in the area, a flat belonging to Barney Simon, a theatre director, who had occasionally made it available for clandestine meetings. On the way there, by sheer coincidence, they came across Simon himself, returning home late at night in his car. He offered his help.

A massive police search was launched. In the morning, AnnMarie was hauled off to the Grays where she endured some aggressive interrogation. Amid the hue and cry, the next night Mannie Brown drove Wolpe and Goldreich to an empty house in Norwood. The following night they were taken to a small cottage in Mountain View. But the cottage was a risky location. It stood in the large grounds of a house belonging to Leon and Maureen Kreel who had previously allowed Communist Party activists to stay there. Denis Goldberg had rented it for several months during 1963. At the time of his arrest, he had left behind a car in the garage and some incriminating documents inside the cottage. Bram had collected the car, driving it miles away before dumping it, while Ralph Sepel picked up the documents. But the danger of discovery remained high.

'We're not happy about putting you here,' Bram told Wolpe and Goldreich when he visited them. 'We have a vague feeling that the police may have got wind of it. We've been unable to come up with anything better than this. Everyone's running shy. We've tried every possible contact, but nobody wants to know.'

Wolpe and Goldreich were instructed to remain 'deadly quiet', giving no sign at all that the cottage was occupied. On the first night after they arrived, they were visited by Bram and Ivan Schermbrucker laden with food. Nightly visits by other members of the escape committee, including Hilda Bernstein in heavy disguise, became a regular event. The Kreels, meanwhile, carried on in the main house as though everything was normal, even throwing a children's party to mark their daughter's third birthday. After hiding in the cottage for 11 days and nights, Wolpe and Goldreich were put into the boot of a car and driven 200 miles to the mission station in Swaziland used by Ezra.

Escape routes were also needed for Umkhonto activists from other parts of the country where the police crackdown was under way. In August, Ronnie Kasrils, a key figure in the Natal regional command which had been broken wide open after the arrest of one its members, Bruno Mtolo, arrived in Johannesburg on the run. Bram arranged for him to hide in a house in Craighall Park temporarily occupied by a young activist he had befriended, John Bizzell, an architect who had recently arrived in Johannesburg from Durban and who knew Kasrils well.

Bram became a regular visitor to the Craighall Park house, trying to work out with Kasrils how Umkhonto operations in Natal might be reorganised. Kasrils recalled in his account of these events: 'The blow to the movement must have placed an immense strain on him, more particularly since it was clear he was shouldering the burden of leading the rearguard action. Yet he remained composed, sprightly and witty during all the times he attended to me.'

Kasrils's girlfriend, Eleanor, also arrived in Johannesburg, anxious to avoid arrest. Her Durban friends insisted she should leave the country, but Bram proposed other plans. 'After long deliberations,' recalled Kasrils, 'Bram asked her to consider going back to Durban because of the role she could play in the reconstruction of the under-ground. It was, admittedly, a risk, but without batting an eye she agreed.' Soon after returning to Durban, Eleanor was arrested by security police.

In prison, Eleanor feigned a mental breakdown and was transferred to a psychiatric hospital. Bram brought the news to Kasrils, along with a letter that Eleanor had managed to smuggle out of hospital, warning that Mtolo was collaborating with the security police, and mentioning the possibility of escape. 'I'm in a lock-up with about 80 poor wretches,' she wrote. 'Some are completely round the bend but it's surprising how quickly one gets used to this sort of thing.' A week or so later she escaped. Once again, Bram brought the news to Kasrils.

'Ronnie went ape,' recalled Bizzell. 'He danced about, climbing over furniture, whooping. Bram grinned, so glad to have brought some good news at last.'

Kasrils and Eleanor were eventually driven across the border into Bechuanaland, together with Julius First who also needed to escape. First's involvement in the Umkhonto network had been exposed as a result of an incident involving the ship he had bought to ferry recruits out of the country. While waiting for instructions to set sail, the ship's captain, Ronnie Fleet, formerly general secretary of the hairdressers' union, held a party on board so raucous that his boat-yard neighbours called the police. After arresting Fleet, the police had gone looking for First at Mannie Brown's office in Johannesburg where he usually worked. Brown managed to put them off, then alerted First who initially went into hiding in a relative's flat before masquerading as a patient at a nursing home.

The ranks of the conspirators and their active supporters were fast dwindling. Ruth First, a member of the Communist Party's central committee, who had often attended meetings at Lilliesleaf, was detained under the 90-day detention laws. The Kreels were arrested and charged with having harboured Goldreich and Wolpe. As the police net tightened, Mannie Brown decided to leave. He went to Beaumont Street to tell Bram. Bram tried to persuade him to go underground instead, but Brown refused and organised his own escape. Among those caught in the net was Jimmy Kantor, Wolpe's brother-in-law and law partner, a criminal lawyer with no political involvement, who was arrested in retaliation for Wolpe's escape.

By making unlimited use of the detention laws, the security police soon broke the back of underground resistance. Subjected to solitary confinement and prolonged interrogation, allowed no visitors or reading material except the Bible, detainees were constantly taunted with the threat that they could be held indefinitely. Their 'cracking point' varied. Writing of her own experiences in prison, Ruth First noted: 'Men holding key positions in the political movement, who had years of hard political experience and sacrifice behind them, cracked like eggshells. Others, with quiet, reticent, self-effacing natures, who had been woolly in making decisions and slow to carry them out, emerged from long spells of isolation shaken but unbroken.' When interrogation methods failed, the police resorted to physical assaults and torture. At first, only 'non-whites' were tortured. Later, whites were included. 'Under torture,' wrote Ben Turok, 'many victims found to their regret that they knew too much and that the police knew that they knew.'

Despite the setbacks, Bram was determined to reconstruct the Communist Party. 'He became more and more obsessed about reconstituting the party,' said Hilda Bernstein, who became his main accomplice at this time. 'He felt he had an obligation, a sense of mission, and he pursued it with absolute fanaticism. He felt the movement had been entrusted to him. He was rigid about it.' Time and again, Bram urged activists to keep the struggle alive, condemning those who opted to accept the government's offer of a one-way exit permit rather than risk imprisonment. Under his leadership a new central committee was established which included Hilda Bernstein, Ivan Schermbrucker, Eli Weinberg and Piet Beyleveld.

Bram was also actively engaged in helping to establish a new high command. He held regular meetings with Wilton Mkwayi, who had replaced Joe Slovo as chief-of-staff, David Kitson and other newly appointed members. The aim now, they agreed, was to build Umkhonto as a network of self-sufficient groups. In addition to all this, following Julius First's departure, Bram took over responsibility for finance. He would often meet Kitson in Greek cafés in Hillbrow, bringing sums of money large enough to purchase cars, vans and other equipment.

But unknown to Bram, the beginning of disaster had already occurred. Seeking new recruits to the Communist Party, members of one of its area committees in Johannesburg decided to invite a young activist, Gerard Ludi, who was well known in radical circles, to join its ranks. Ludi was in fact a police spy. Normally the cell system used by the communists provided a high degree of security. Strict discipline was required. Apart from one key figure, members of one cell knew little or nothing about the work of other cells or who its members were. Ludi was attached to a 'young persons' group' involved in nothing more subversive than slogan-painting. But by chance it was a cell that Bram occasionally attended.

An undergraduate at the University of the Witwatersrand, Ludi had joined the security police in December 1960 and was given the task of infiltrating left-wing organisations. Masquerading as a freelance journalist, he ingratiated himself with staff at the Johannesburg office of *New Age* where Ruth First was the editor and Ivan Schermbrucker the manager. A lean, dark-haired man, with a thin face, a goatee beard and an engaging manner, he joined the Congress of Democrats and befriended a large number of left-wing activists. He went to parties at the Fischers and the Slovos, and became particularly attached to Toni Bernstein, the daughter of Rusty and Hilda. By regularly participating in protest meetings, study circles and volunteer groups involved in slogan-painting and leaflet distribution, he soon gained sufficient trust to be given a minor role in the Congress hierarchy. On one occasion, he was arrested after putting up posters at night, further enhancing his reputation. With the help of senior Congress members, Ludi and Toni Bernstein were sent as delegates to a Moscow Peace Conference in July 1962. On his return to Johannesburg, Ludi reported back to a specially convened secret meeting in Mannie Brown's house. Bram, Hilda Bernstein and Mannie Brown were present. As with everything else he did, Ludi passed on information of this meeting to security police headquarters.

In May 1963, in the first breakthrough the security police made in penetrating the Communist Party, Ludi was invited to become a member by Jean Middleton, an area group leader in charge of a number of volunteer groups in Johannesburg. Middleton herself had misgivings about Ludi. She found him, as she said, 'shifty-eyed'. But he was recommended for membership by a wide range of members, young and old, including Joe Slovo.

Ludi's first cell meeting was held in Middleton's flat in Hillbrow two days later. Apart from Middleton, two other members were present, Ann Nicholson, a lively and attractive arts student, and Florence Duncan, a radiographer who had recently arrived in Johannesburg from Cape Town. Two other members were expected but did not arrive. Ludi was told of the various rules and regulations, and asked to choose a cover name. He took the name of Harry.

A week later, Ludi attended his second cell meeting, held again in Middleton's flat. There was a knock at the door and, to Ludi's amazement, in walked Bram. Bram proceeded to chair the meeting.

He welcomed Ludi to 'the family' and then, according to Ludi, went on to warn cell members about the dangers of police infiltration. Bram participated in several subsequent cell meetings that Ludi attended, stressing the need for party activists to stand firm. At one meeting, according to Ludi, he read out a directive from the central committee which said: 'Do not run. Stick to your posts and don't let police oppression intimidate you.'

In June, two weeks before the police raid on Lilliesleaf, Ludi told the Johannesburg newspaper for which he was working of an illicit radio broadcast he had heard at a party member's flat made by Walter Sisulu, then in hiding from the police, defiantly proclaiming the ANC's determination to fight on against the government. When the newspaper subsequently published a report about the broadcast, Ludi was questioned by the police. To enhance his credentials, he decided to make a fuss about 'police intimidation' at the next cell meeting he attended. Middleton advised him to consult Bram.

Accompanied by Ann Nicholson, Ludi drove to Beaumont Street, parking his car some distance from the house. Bram questioned him sharply about what security measures they had taken in getting to Beaumont Street, and then led them into the lounge where Molly sat reading.

Ludi explained his predicament: he was concerned the police might take action against him, and asked whether he should avoid such contentious stories in the future. Not at all, replied Bram, according to Ludi; it would have been better if he had been arrested, then the movement could have gained some favourable publicity. He added that if Ludi was imprisoned in future he should do everything he could to obstruct prison officials, perhaps even going on a hunger strike.

Shortly after these events, Ludi was transferred to a newspaper in Cape Town. While he was there, suspicions about him were raised by Mannie Brown. Just before he fled the country, Mannie was hauled in for interrogation by the security police and asked about the secret meeting at his house that Ludi had attended on his return from Moscow. He deduced that Ludi was the source of information. Ludi was suspended from the party for three months, yet was then allowed to renew his place in Jean Middleton's cell.

CHAPTER 8

THE RIVONIA TRIAL

For three months the Rivonia conspirators were held in solitary confinement in small cells for 23 hours a day, without access to lawyers and with only the Bible to read. 'I have been keeping a record and find that I am averaging 18 spoken words a day,' Rusty Bernstein said in a note smuggled out to his wife, Hilda. '"Thank you" three times for meals. "May I have a match, please?" twice at exercise times.'

The government meanwhile induced a mood of fear and hysteria among the white community. Ministers and police officials openly proclaimed the detainees guilty of violence and bloodshed, even though none had been charged with any offence. When Hilda Bernstein went in search of an attorney willing to help defend her husband, she encountered one rejection after another. The hazards for any lawyer acting on behalf of the Rivonia conspirators were severe, at both a professional and a social level. Those she approached reacted with polite excuses: 'I really am too busy.' Discussing the problem with Bram, he suggested she should try a young attorney named Joel Joffe.

Joffe, however, was in the process of closing his law practice. Like an increasing number of young white professional people, he had made plans to emigrate. Though not politically active, he had grown to dislike the repressive nature of life in South Africa. When Hilda Bernstein contacted him, he was sceptical about what could be achieved. 'She was asking that I should embark on a case of unknown duration in the defence of people I did not know, whose actions I knew nothing about and on a charge which had not been formulated,' said Joffe. 'I felt that even if I were to agree, it would be a waste of time.' Any trial would merely be a formality, he assumed, given the evidence the government claimed to have. Nevertheless he was sufficiently appalled by the manner in which Hilda Bernstein had been shunned by his fellow lawyers that he decided to postpone his family's departure for Australia to take on the case. Within a few weeks the families of other detainees approached him for help as well.

Though Joffe was unable to ascertain from either the security police or state prosecutors what charges might be brought against the detainees, he learned that they were hard at work preparing a prosecution and he began to assemble a defence team. The obvious starting point seemed to be Bram Fischer. All the families of detainees who visited Joffe had suggested that he should try to get Bram's services for their defence. Joffe knew of Bram as a fearless radical lawyer, friendly with government opponents, who was nevertheless widely admired in the legal profession.

'He had a charm, a great gentleness and a personal sincerity which endeared him to everybody,' recalled Joffe. 'But he also had the other qualities of outstanding men – a painstaking, conscientious mind, a clear insight, tremendous drive and ability, singleness of purpose and immense courage and integrity. Bram was the most popular man at the Johannesburg Bar. Nobody had hard words to say about him though some had harsh words for his politics.'

What neither Joffe nor anyone outside a small group of conspirators knew was Bram's involvement in the sabotage campaign and his role as an underground communist leader. His political sympathies were clear, but not his part in clandestine activity. When Joffe approached Bram seeking his help in defending the Rivonia detainees, he had not the slightest inkling of what he was really asking Bram to do.

For Bram, the dilemma was only too obvious. He knew that the evidence obtained by the security police at Lilliesleaf was likely to implicate him: his handwriting and fingerprints were on several documents seized there. He also realised that during the trial he would be called upon to examine witnesses, like the black farm-workers at Lilliesleaf, detained by police, who could betray him at any moment. He offered to assist Joffe in preparing the defence case, but expressed reluctance to become part of the defence team at the trial. He pointed out that in order to undermine the defence team the police might arrest him, and suggested that Joffe should turn to other advocates to ensure that the defence of the accused was safeguarded.

'In the atmosphere then existing in South Africa it was not at all farfetched to imagine the arrest or detention – with or without charge –

of Bram Fischer,' said Joffe. 'We all felt that Bram might be whipped off at any moment. It was therefore necessary for us to assemble a team for the defence which would not be crippled should it be summarily removed. We discussed the people at the Johannesburg Bar. There were not many candidates for such a job who would be either willing or suitable.'

Joffe recruited two other advocates. One was George Bizos, a Greek-born lawyer who as a boy had fled with his father to escape the Nazi invasion, and who in South Africa had become well known for his involvement in political trials. The other was Arthur Chaskalson, a talented young advocate who had no political associations but a deep commitment to the defence of people who would otherwise have gone undefended.

With the prospect of a trial growing closer, the three young defence lawyers, Bizos, Chaskalson and Joffe, exerted tremendous pressure on Bram to agree to lead the defence team. Chaskalson argued that no other advocate could put so well the argument that the conspirators had done no more than the Afrikaner rebels who had taken up arms against the government in 1914 and who had received prison sentences rather than the death penalty. Only an Afrikaner of Bram's standing would be able to convince an Afrikaner judge of that, he said.

Bram at first held out, claiming that he had too many other commitments. But eventually he agreed to lead the defence team and persuaded an old communist friend, Vernon Berrangé, with whom he had worked during the treason trial and who was much feared for his rapier-like skills at cross-examination, to join him. Though his colleagues had no idea of the risks Bram was taking, the Rivonia conspirators understood only too well. When Rusty Bernstein first heard that Bram would be acting on their behalf in the trial, he turned to the others and said: 'He deserves the Victoria Cross.'

Yet still Joffe could obtain no definite information about who the defendants might be and what charges they might face. On 7 October, hearing rumours on the legal grapevine that the conspirators were due to appear in court the following day, Joffe phoned Percy Yutar, the deputy attorney-general of the Transvaal who had been appointed to lead the prosecution, to ask if this was so, and was advised to be in the Supreme Court in Pretoria at ten o'clock the next morning.

As Bram was occupied with another case that day, Joffe, Bizos and Chaskalson travelled to Pretoria without him, only to find that no one at the Supreme Court knew anything about the case. From the attorney-general, Rudolf Rhein, they managed to ascertain that the case would begin on the following day, but they were still not told who the defendants were or what the charges were, merely that they would find the defendants in Pretoria Local prison.

After lengthy arguments over whether white and black prisoners could mix, the prison authorities eventually produced 11 defendants. Into the interview room came seven Rivonia conspirators: Walter Sisulu, Govan Mbeki, Kathy Kathrada, Raymond Mhlaba, Denis Goldberg, Rusty Bernstein and Bob Hepple. Two others, Elias Motsoaledi and Andrew Mlangeni, were junior Umkhonto members, who had been arrested before the Rivonia raid.

To their delight and astonishment Nelson Mandela arrived, accompanied by guards. He had been brought to Pretoria from Robben Island soon after the Rivonia raid in July and held, like the others, in solitary confinement. In the year since he had begun his five-year prison sentence, his large frame had withered; he looked thin and underweight. His face had a sallow complexion, his cheeks were sunken, and the skin under his eyes hung in bags. But his mood on seeing his friends was buoyant. His fellow prisoners gathered round in jubilation, talking and laughing.

'They were drunk with speech, with human communication and contact, with being able to talk, to meet with and touch other people,' recalled Joel Joffe.

The sense of reunion was not shared by all the defendants. Among their number was James Kantor, Wolpe's brother-in-law. Normally an ebullient and cheerful figure, after two months of solitary confinement he was in a state of shock, his face haggard and drawn, his extrovert nature crushed. His law practice had disintegrated. All the accused knew that he had had nothing to do with their conspiracy. He had been arrested out of sheer vindictiveness for the escape of his brother-in-law Harold Wolpe, and put into the trial as his proxy. Everyone urged him to arrange a separate defence.

One of the Rivonia conspirators, Bob Hepple, was also in a serious predicament. His role in the underground movement had been at a secondary level, arranging meetings, passing messages and funds, acting as a courier. On the day of the police raid at Rivonia, he had gone there on secretariat business. During solitary confinement, police interrogators had taunted him with a copy of Operation Mayibuye, telling him he was certain to be sentenced to death unless he collaborated. Hepple thought the whole plan was madness. 'I didn't want to die for Operation Mayibuye,' he said later. To the dismay of his fellow prisoners, he told them he had been asked to give evidence against them and that he was still considering what to do. Then he left the room.

After leaving the men's section of Pretoria Local, the three lawyers proceeded to the women's section, demanding to see Ruth First whom they had heard might be included in the trial. They were refused permission, and left the prison with some relief since it meant that she was unlikely to be charged along with the Rivonia conspirators. Bram's view was that the government would not want to put on trial a white women accused of crimes that carried the death penalty.

The following day, 9 October, Bram drove from Johannesburg to the Supreme Court on Church Square, an ornate nineteenth-century building with columns, marble facings and brass rails, known as the Palace of Justice. Armed police were everywhere, packed into the square outside and stationed in every lobby, every corridor and doorway inside the court building. Inside the courtroom itself, security police filled the white public benches.

A mile away from the court, an armed convoy escorting the prisoners in a special van set out from Pretoria Local, sweeping across road intersections guarded by police and driving through the tall iron-grille gates into the back yard of the courthouse. From the basement cells, Mandela, dressed in shabby prison garb, short trousers, a khaki shirt and sandals, led the procession of prisoners up the steps into the courtroom, raising a clenched fist as he emerged. He had lost so much weight and his skin was so pallid from prison life that to friends in the spectators' gallery he seemed almost unrecognisable. Most of the other defendants looked haggard and drawn.

At ten o'clock the judge assigned to the case, Quartus de Wet, judge-president of the Transvaal, a moody, complex character with a reputation for being self-willed, obstinate, and impatient with legal quibbles, took his place. Percy Yutar rose to call 'the case of the state against the National High Command' and, for the first time, produced an indictment, handing one copy to the court and passing another to Bram. The accused were charged under the *Suppression of Communism Act* and the *Sabotage Act*, which carried the death penalty, with complicity in more than 200 acts of sabotage in preparation for guerrilla warfare, armed invasion and violent revolution. In addition to the defendants in court, the indictment listed 24 co-conspirators including Wolpe, Goldreich, Slovo, Hodgson, Kotane and Harmel.

Bram immediately rose to apply for an adjournment. The accused, he said, were facing charges of the utmost gravity, which could involve the death penalty. The indictment was a complex document alleging a large number of separate acts in almost every part of South Africa, citing co-conspirators and agents scattered not only throughout the country but abroad. He added that the accused, after being held in solitary confinement for three months, were not in a fit state either to instruct counsel or to consider their defence adequately, before a period of recuperation. 'In the Criminal Code, solitary confinement has always been very carefully regulated. No more than two days' solitary confinement and spare diet per week is allowed ... These accused have been in confinement for 88 days.' He went on: 'There is an old saying that justice must not only be done, but must be seen to be done. The accused in this case are people who carry the deep respect of a very large proportion of the population, and for this reason alone justice should be seen to be done. There should be no urgency to bring them to trial. We want justice to be seen to be done.' He asked for an adjournment of six weeks.

Yutar jumped in to oppose any postponement. In a high-pitched voice, he spoke of witnesses who had to be called before the end of the month, adding, with a theatrical flourish: 'I fear for their safety.' The judge decided that a three-week period was sufficient, and adjourned the court until 29 October.

Immediately after the adjournment, the court reconvened to hear a bail application from Kantor. The case against Kantor was so flimsy that his lawyers were convinced he would have no difficulty in obtaining bail. Yutar intervened, however, to claim that he had been fully involved in the conspiracy, and the judge consequently denied him bail.

During the three-week adjournment, Bram drove himself relentlessly, preparing his arguments with meticulous care and thoroughness. 'Bram is still working himself to death,' Molly wrote to Ruth. 'Heaven knows how he manages it. He is carrying most of the burden of the Rivonia Trial and lots of other people's burdens too. I mean everyone comes to him for comfort and advice – so if we both turn into alcoholics you'll know the reason why.'

Bram's massive workload added to Molly's growing sense of loneliness. She particularly felt the loss of so many of her friends, who had gone either into exile or to prison or who were subjected to banning orders and house arrest. She tended to keep away from other friends to avoid incriminating them. After a long day, Bram would return home for dinner, snatch a glance at a newspaper and then, even when he was exhausted, head upstairs to his study to work late into the night. Molly was sometimes found doing a crossword puzzle on her own, chain-smoking. Both of them drank fairly heavily.

The focus of Bram's attention was the indictment. It contained vague and general allegations, making it impossible to discern precisely what the offence was, by whom it had been committed and in what way the accused either individually or jointly were alleged to be connected with it. The defence team therefore decided to ask the prosecution for 'further particulars', sending over a long list of questions, seeking to clarify which of the accused or co-conspirators were alleged to have carried out each of the acts of sabotage listed in the indictment; how the conspiracy had been entered into; and when and where and on what date it was alleged that each member of the National High Command had become a member.

The replies they received were curt: either 'These facts are known' or 'These facts are peculiarly within the knowledge of the accused.' Joel Joffe remarked: 'The prosecution was clearly following a simple precept: "You are guilty. Therefore you know what you did. Therefore we don't have to tell you."' The defence accordingly decided to move in court for the dismissal of the indictment.

The task fell to Bram. Conscious that the lives of his own friends and colleagues depended on his conduct of the case, he picked his words with care, hesitating to ensure he chose precisely the right word, thinking slowly and deliberately between sentences, sometimes pausing for long periods after making one point before framing the next. He delivered his arguments in a quiet, methodical manner, lacking any sense of drama, but exposing the defects of the indictment one by one, with devastating clarity.

Some of the sabotage acts, he said, had been committed before any *Sabotage Act* existed in South Africa, and therefore could not be offences in terms of the Act under which the accused had been charged. He pointed out that Mandela had been charged with having committed 156 acts of sabotage which had taken place while he was in prison. He ridiculed the lack of particularity and the unsatisfactory answers given when the defence had asked for further particulars.

'The acts of sabotage set out in the indictment may have been committed by other people and not by the accused. But the state refuses to tell us the names of the people who it alleges committed the acts. Unless the state says who carried out each of the acts, how is the defence to meet the charges? Either the state knows who committed the acts, or it does not. If it does not know, then it should not charge them with the acts. If it does know, it should tell us.'

If the state with all the resources available to it was not able to furnish the accused with the necessary particulars of the allegations then how, he asked, was it possible that the accused with their limited resources should be expected to discover the necessary particulars and fill them in for themselves? There was only one explanation of an indictment such as this: the state had decided that the accused were guilty, and since they were guilty a defence would be a waste of time.

Bram's crushing exposure of the indictment was followed by further scorn from Kantor's counsellor, George Lowen. In Kantor's case, he argued, it was even more necessary than usual for the prosecution to state the basis of its claims fully and clearly. Kantor was not being tried for what he himself had done, but was being held vicariously responsible for what had been done by his partner. Yet the prosecution's response to questions seeking information of the charges Kantor faced had been 'ludicrous', he said. 'Take, for example, question five. The answer given by the state is: "dash, dash, dash, exclamation mark!"' At this point, the judge, who had been showing increasing signs of irritation and impatience with the proceedings, remarked acidly: "In my copy there are four dashes, Mr Lowen."

When Lowen had finished, the judge turned to Hepple, who was unrepresented, to ask whether he wished to say anything about the indictment. But before Hepple had time to reply, Yutar sprang to his feet to announce that all charges against Hepple were being withdrawn, adding, with a note of triumph, that he would be the first witness for the state against the accused. Hepple turned pale, stood up and was escorted down the stairs to the police cells below.

Despite the sensation over Hepple's defection, Yutar was still left with an indictment virtually in tatters. With increasing desperation, he resorted to 'begging' and 'imploring' the court not to reject the indictment, promising to provide whatever particulars were required to make a sound indictment. De Wet replied testily that it was not his responsibility to tell the state what particulars were required to make a good indictment and, ignoring further pleading by Yutar, he threw out the indictment. Technically, the prisoners were free men. But amid pandemonium in the court, security police rushed forward to re-arrest them and hustled them down to the cells.

'Life is absolutely fascinating if one is strong enough to take it,' Molly wrote to Ruth from Beaumont Street at the end of one Sunday in November.

Take today for instance. Stanley Uys [a well-known journalist] came to breakfast. Then I fetched the Slovo children to spend the day and served tea to the Berrangés. Then the representatives of the BBC and the *Daily Telegraph* turned up. Then I gave lunch to Bram and Paul and the Slovo children and three unexpected guests. In between some swimmers had been. Then at 2.30, four lawyers arrived for a consultation on the Looksmart inquest [into the death of Looksmart Ngudle, an ANC prisoner who died in detention] and at 3.30, four others arrived to work on the Rivonia Trial which restarts tomorrow. Then Harold Hanson and his junior turned up. They are appearing for Kantor tomorrow. Then I had to dash to the airport terminal to fetch a 6ft 4ins English MP and advocate who has come out as an observer for the Rivonia Trial. In between, more swimmers, more teas, more drinks. Then the said observer stayed to supper and Stanley Uys dropped in as well and had to sup off salads as he wasn't expected and I only had cold meats besides.

In addition to all this, there had been the 'odd half dozen people who came to see Bram urgently "for literally two minutes"'.

As well as coping with an endless stream of visitors to Beaumont Street, Molly was involved in looking after the needs of prisoners and their families and in helping Bram with research for the trial. She often attended the trial, sitting beside Hilda Bernstein. As Hilda later wrote: 'Molly is constantly busy with the trial, and Bram relies on her tremendously. She shoulders a great burden of work. Only Bram knows how much he depends on her.'

Yet the strains were beginning to tell. Both Bram and Molly were desperately worried about the outcome of the trial, about how much the fate of the conspirators depended on Bram's skill in court. Bram sometimes spent sleepless nights in anguish at the possibility of a death sentence. Adding to the tension were the hazards of their clandestine work at Beaumont Street, dealing with surreptitious visitors arriving at the back gate, engaging in whispered conversations in the garden, hiding documents and money, always alert to the risk of a police raid. On one occasion, Esmé Goldberg, the wife of Denis Goldberg, was arrested at the Fischers' swimming pool. 'Life is too depressing,' Molly wrote to Ilse in Cape Town. 'Heaven only knows how they knew she was here.' When Ruth, who was working in London, wrote to Molly to say she was thinking of coming home at the end of the year, depending on what their plans were, Molly remarked in a letter: 'Poor dear. She doesn't realise that we don't "plan", but only live from day to day.'

Their moments of pleasure were rare. When Ruth wrote from London announcing her engagement to Anthony Eastwood, a Rhodesian lawyer she had met at Cape Town University, Bram replied that it had been 'the best day for us' in more than three months. 'Your mother wept. I don't think you've ever seen her weep. She weeps in a way that no one can see it. And the significance of her weeping has nothing to do with Anthony. The last time she wept like this was when she decided (after many years of tempestuous consideration) to marry me. I don't blame her ...'

Despite his customary calmness and composure, Bram too was showing increasing signs of tension. Pat Davidson, who had known the Fischers since childhood and who came to stay at Beaumont Street at this time while on probation as a public prosecutor, noticed how his anger showed more often. 'He became impatient with journalists and quite intolerant of people who he thought were ignorant. He didn't like criticism of communism. His face flushed red. He became angry about the government, angry about reports of prisoners being tortured, angry about white indifference. But otherwise he was very controlled and very disciplined. And he was still warm and caring. Even in moments of great stress, he was still concerned about how other people were feeling. He had an enormous influence on anyone who came into contact with him. People wanted to live up to what he thought of you.'

The risks he took were becoming ever higher. While waiting for state prosecutors to file a new indictment against the Rivonia prisoners, Bram arranged to meet the defector Bob Hepple who had been released on bail and who was due to appear as the prosecution's first witness. Aware of the danger that they were both being followed by security police, Bram met Hepple three times in hotels in Johannes-burg, persuaded him to escape the country and then, with Ivan Schermbrucker's help, proceeded to make the arrangements to get him away. 'The risk to Bram,' said Hepple, 'was huge.'

But Bram would not let up. Even with the burden of all his other work, he became involved in drawing up a new appraisal of the Communist Party's prospects entitled *Time for Reassessment*. The aim was to give members an outline of the party's strategy, a guide on operational methods and some form of warning about the difficulties they might experience in detention, gleaned over the months from former detainees. Bram was particularly keen that supporters should be prepared in advance for the rigours of detention. 'Bram schooled me,' said John Bizzell. 'He told me, assume you will be arrested, be prepared for it. He instructed me on how to get messages in and out of prison, how to conceal messages on sheets of toilet paper in the laundry, how to conceal paper and pencils in the soles of slippers, how to handle prison life.'

Reviewing the future, the paper warned:

We must assume that the government's attack will continue and will not lessen. Many courageous people are being prosecuted in long-drawn-out trials. Heavy sentences must be anticipated, and those in power will probably keep people in jail even when they have served the sentences imposed on them ...

Nevertheless, we have reached a stage where we can survey the situation, examine the enemy and his weapons, and plan methods to defend ourselves against those weapons and to take steps to defeat them. To do this will require hard work, clear thinking, patience and courage. But it can and will be achieved through the application of our scientific methods that teach us to learn from the past; to know that we live in ever-changing, not static circumstances; to understand the forces at work; to make use of those which are emerging and to destroy those that are dying. The new forces are those of liberation; the dying forces are those represented by the Nationalist barbarians.

The paper went on to pinpoint all the failures and faults of the past, the slipshod underground methods that had been used, the carelessness and lack of planning.

People were recruited for work, and sometimes very dangerous work, without adequate preparation, merely because they were willing, without regard to their ability in the future to resist solitary confinement and torture.

To resist torture, people must be strong and brave, and must prepare themselves in advance to withstand it by realising what lies ahead of them if they are arrested; by preparing themselves mentally and resolving not to answer questions or make statements under any circumstances.

Much emphasis was placed on Bram's speciality – security. Under the heading, 'Rigid discipline – rigid security', the paper declared:

Security must be carefully planned, constantly discussed, continuously revised.

Every single individual must know from now on that he is not playing a game; he is not conducting a mere pretence; he is involved in what truly is a matter of life and death. The practice of having one person in every group or committee whose job it is

90

to check constantly on discipline and security must be applied rigidly ...

Every meeting, every act must be planned to the last possible detail, to be carried out with split-second timing and efficiency. No evidence of any kind must be left. Nothing must be put down on paper unless absolutely necessary. Political documents, study books or leaflets must never be kept where police might possibly raid or search.

Fingerprints must not be left anywhere – on paper, machines, glasses, furniture, doors, etc. ...

It is easier to be followed on foot than in a car. The fact that you cannot see anyone watching you is no guarantee of safety. Your actions can be seen by someone hidden in a house or building quite a long way from you. People watching or following others do not look like the usual SB [Special Branch] types.

The delivery man, the butcher boy, the street sweeper in overalls, the neighbour, the woman shopping – you must be as careful of these as you would if they appeared in police uniform.

You can be listened to by microphones hidden in houses or motor-cars, or by instruments that can pick up your voices over long distances. Tiny transmitters can be concealed behind the lapels of someone's jacket, in a case or in a book.

Use disguises where necessary. Your unit must discuss and experiment. Sometimes something very simple such as a hat or small item of dress may make the difference.

As soon as someone was arrested, special precautions had to be taken. No one was to be regarded as wholly reliable.

A copy of the document quickly found its way into the hands of the security police. Shortly after the police spy, Gerard Ludi, had been cleared to work again with Jean Middleton, he was summoned to her Hillbrow flat to study the document. When he arrived there she had visitors, so she gave it to him and told him to read it by himself. Ludi walked out of her flat, handed the document for photocopying to the security police waiting nearby, then returned it to Jean Middleton half an hour later. So interested were the security police in the activities in Middleton's flat that they placed an agent permanently in an adjacent flat, with recording apparatus to monitor conversations there and a one-way window on the front door to keep a check on who visited it.

Back at the Supreme Court, the prosecution produced another indictment. Bram considered it to be as defective as the previous one, and applied again for its dismissal. But this time De Wet was in no mood to countenance further delay, and ordered the case to proceed.

On 3 December 1963 the trial began. The accused pleaded not guilty. 'The government,' said Mandela, 'should be in the dock, not me.' Then Yutar rose to give his opening address. Without bothering to consult defence counsel, he had arranged for it to be recorded by the state-controlled radio network: a small black microphone had appeared overnight in front of his desk. Bram intervened to demand its removal, and De Wet concurred.

As Yutar began to outline the full extent of the conspiracy, the defence team was left considerably shaken. He gave details of the Rivonia headquarters, the arsenal at Travallyn, the plans for training in sabotage and guerrilla warfare, and the contents of Operation Mayibuye with its aims of violent insurrection. Though Bram was well prepared for this, the others suddenly realised for the first time what they were facing.

'From that moment on, we saw the case in a very simple light,' recalled Joffe. 'For most of the accused the only possible verdict was "guilty". The case was therefore, as far as we were concerned, a battle to prevent the death sentence being carried out.'

CHAPTER 9

THE VERDICT

During the next three months, the prosecution presented scores of witnesses, hundreds of documents, photographs and maps, and a whole library of captured books on guerrilla warfare. Bram took advantage of being handed lists of sabotage targets and maps by the prosecution in the normal course of court proceedings by passing them on to David Kitson during their clandestine meetings in Greek cafés in Hillbrow for further use.

At the opening stages of the trial, when the prosecution chose to lead off with a series of minor witnesses, including the domestic servants and farm labourers at Lilliesleaf who had been held in detention for five months, Bram managed to avoid being identified by making sure he was engaged in other legal business elsewhere when they appeared in court.

But other witnesses were not so easily handled. One whom Bram had to confront was Patrick Mthembu, a senior Umkhonto member who had been trained in China and who had worked closely with all the main conspirators including Bram. After two spells in solitary confinement, Mthembu agreed to give evidence in exchange for indemnity. At any moment during his testimony he could have given Bram up. But though he revealed much to implicate the accused, he made no mention of Bram.

The state's key witness was Bruno Mtolo, Ronnie Kasrils's colleague in the Natal regional command, a Communist Party member who had defected within hours of his arrest in August 1963. Mtolo gave evidence against Nelson Mandela, whom he had met in Durban in 1962, and several other leading conspirators whom he had encountered during a visit he made to Lilliesleaf in 1963 – Slovo, Sisulu and Mbeki – but not, fortunately, Bram.

Bram also had to endure the court's examination of a number of incriminating documents. One document, identified by a handwriting expert as being written by Harold Wolpe, was passed by the prosecutor in court to Bram, who looked at it without a trace of concern and then passed it to the rest of the team who, aghast, saw only too clearly that it had been written by Bram himself. The prosecution produced other examples of Bram's handwriting but chose, for reasons of convenience, not to identify them. Yutar would simply say: 'There is a document here, my Lord, which is in somebody else's handwriting.'

For the duration of the trial, Bram had acquired a form of immunity. 'He felt the security police would be reluctant to arrest the leading counsel in the Rivonia Trial while the trial lasted,' recalled Hilda Bernstein who sat through the proceedings day by day. But no one – including Bram – expected this immunity to last when it was over.

In their consultations with the conspirators, the defence team had to go to extraordinary lengths to avoid surveillance by the security police. Provided with a consulting room on the ground floor of Pretoria Local prison, they assumed that the room was bugged and resorted to communicating with one another by using a simple coded language. Nelson Mandela always referred to Bram, with a tilt of his head and a lowering of the hand, as 'the short one'. They also wrote down messages, taking care to burn them in ashtrays before their daily sessions were over. Prison warders watched this procedure through a window with some irritation. Before long, a notorious security policeman, Theunis Swanepoel, was seen pacing the corridor and glancing through a window in the door whenever he passed. Realising how badly Swanepoel wanted to get his hands on their messages, they laid a trap for him. On a piece of paper, Govan Mbeki wrote: 'It's so nice to have Lieutenant Swanepoel with us again', waited for Swanepoel to pass by, and then passed it ostentatiously to Joffe. Joffe studied the message for some time, whispered in a conspiratorial manner to the prisoners and then, placing the message in an ashtray, fumbled for his matches. Swanepoel dashed into the room, seized the ashtray with the message in it, and rushed outside. He did not appear outside the door again.

Halfway through the trial the prison authorities provided a new consultation room specially constructed for the purpose. It was long and narrow, and down the middle of it prison building staff had installed a wooden partition and a heavy metal grating, dividing the room into two. Bar stools were placed on either side, one side for the lawyers, the other for the conspirators. When the lawyers were first ushered into the new consultation room, the prisoners were already seated on the other side of the counter, lined up in a long row like customers at a milk bar. Mandela stood, smiled politely and said: 'What will it be today, gentlemen? Chocolate or ice-cream soda?'

The lawyers protested that the arrangements, with nine accused in a single line along the counter on one side and five lawyers sitting on bar stools on the other, made a proper consultation virtually impossible. The only way for each lawyer to be heard by all the accused was to shout. Debate of any kind was out of the question. Even when the prisoners tried sitting shoulder-to-shoulder, one end of the line remained some 20 feet away from the other end. Exhibits and notes had to be slid through a tiny space under the bars of the grating, and could only be seen by prisoners one at a time.

But their protests were ignored. Once again, they all had to assume that the new contraption contained listening devices relaying everything that was said to officials outside. And once again they resorted to passing notes on any issue considered important.

The routine that Bram and the other lawyers followed was to make the 30-mile journey to Pretoria early in the morning, to arrive there by 9 am when they were permitted entry into the prison. At noon they had to leave for two hours while the prisoners were given lunch. Then they spent another two hours in consultations in the afternoon, before driving back to Johannesburg where they continued working until the early hours of the morning, usually at Beaumont Street.

Even at Beaumont Street, they took extreme precautions to avoid surveillance. During daytime, they tended to work outside in the garden to escape bugging devices placed in the house. At night, they turned on a radio to drown their discussion, or passed messages, or stepped outside.

In March, the prosecution completed its case. Jimmy Kantor, against whom no evidence had been produced, was discharged. With his personal and professional life in ruins, he made plans to emigrate. One by one, other friends of Bram decided to leave. Among them was Ruth First, interrogated while held for 117 days in solitary confinement. Her ordeal had led to an attempted suicide. On her release in December 1963, she had gone round to Beaumont Street to talk to Bram about what she should do, whether to go or to stay, sitting in the bathroom with the bath tap running to drown out their discussion. Bram wanted her to stay but said she should make up her own mind. She felt like a deserter, but the hazards and insecurity of life in South Africa had become too great for her and she accepted the government's offer of a one-way exit permit. Her decision to go in March was a grievous blow to the dwindling band of conspirators.

'I was deeply affected by Ruth's departure,' said Hilda Bernstein. 'She was a close friend. I knew of the prison agony that brought her near death, and believed she should go. At the same time I was being deserted. It was not just a personal matter. She had been an intimate part of the years of struggle, and now she was forced to relinquish it; South Africa would be the poorer. It seemed a personal loss, and something much bigger. So many had left, so many more would have to go.'

On 20 April 1964, Bram commenced the case for the defence. During their discussions with the defence team in prison, the conspirators had been clear about their objective in the trial. They wanted to turn it into a showcase against the government, giving them the opportunity to explain to the world their reasons for embarking on a campaign of violence, and the circumstances which had forced them to do so. They were not interested in seeking to lessen their punishment. They therefore intended to admit initiating the sabotage campaign and making contingency plans for guerrilla warfare if the sabotage campaign failed to change the government's mind. But they would deny that they had already decided to embark on guerrilla warfare, as the prosecution contended. They therefore needed to clarify the circumstances under which Operation Mayibuye was drawn up. They would not attempt to refute evidence obtained by the prosecution that they knew to be true, but they would refuse to provide further evidence.

To ensure that the court heard a clear and coherent account of their political aims and ideals, the accused decided that Mandela should lead off the defence case by reading a statement from the dock, unhindered by cross-examination or by questions from the bench. Mandela spent about two weeks working on the draft, mainly in his cell in the evenings, and then showed it to fellow prisoners and to Bram. Bram was worried about its forthright tone and took it to a colleague, Harold Hanson, a much respected advocate, for his opinion. 'If Mandela reads this in court,' Hanson told Bram, 'they will take him straight out to the back of the courthouse and string him up.' Bram urged Mandela to modify the speech, but to no avail. 'I felt we were likely to hang no matter what we said, so we might as well say what we truly believed,' said Mandela. 'Bram begged me not to read the final paragraph, but I was adamant.'

In his opening address to the court, delivered in his customary quiet and calm manner, Bram announced that certain aspects of the state's evidence would be conceded by the accused but that other parts would be challenged. The accused would deny, as the prosecution had claimed, that Umkhonto was 'the military wing' of the African National Congress – a charge that could have made ANC members liable to prosecution for sabotage or treason. They would seek to show how instead the ANC had tried to keep the two organisations separate. They would also deny emphatically that the ANC was 'a tool' of the Communist Party, with the same aims and objectives. Of particular importance, the accused would deny that Umkhonto had taken the decision to proceed with Operation Mayibuye and embark upon guerrilla warfare.

De Wet: Will that be denied?

Fischer: That will be denied. Here the evidence will show that while preparations for guerrilla warfare were being made from as early as 1962, no plan was ever adopted, and the evidence will show why it was hoped throughout that such a step could be avoided. In regard to the last issue, the court will be asked to have regard to the motives, the character and political background of the men in charge of Umkhonto we Sizwe and its operations. In other words, to have regard amongst other things to the tradition of non-violence of the African National Congress; to have regard to the reasons which led these men to resort to sabotage in an attempt to achieve their political objectives, and why, in the light of these facts, they are to be believed when they say that 'Operation Mayibuye' had not been adopted, and that they would not have adopted it while there was some chance, however remote, of having their objectives achieved by the combination of mass political struggle and sabotage.

Bram paused at this point while the judges finished making notes, and then continued:

The defence case, my Lord, will commence with a statement from the dock by Nelson Mandela, who personally took part in the establishment of Umkhonto, and who will be able to inform the court of the beginnings of that organisation and of its history up to August 1962 when he was arrested.

Yutar was caught by surprise. He assumed he would have the benefit of cross-examining Mandela. As Mandela rose slowly, Yutar jumped to his feet, his shrill voice rising in complaint. 'My Lord! My Lord! I think you should warn the accused that what he says from the dock has far less weight than if he submitted himself to cross-examination!'

The judge looked at him sourly and replied: 'I think, Mr Yutar, that counsel for the defence have sufficient experience to be able to advise their clients without your assistance.'

Standing in the dock, Mandela began reading his statement slowly and with calm deliberation, his voice carrying clearly across the courtroom. He outlined the reasons behind the formation of Umkhonto, pointing out that all lawful methods of expressing opposition to white supremacy had been closed by legislation, and explained why he thought that sabotage might induce the government to change course. He discussed the activities at Lilliesleaf, examined the relationship between the ANC and the Communist Party, and went on to clarify the African objectives of equal political rights and a 'just share' in the whole of South Africa.

For five hours, Mandela continued reading his statement. Then he put down his papers and turned to face the judge, speaking his final words from memory:

During my lifetime I have dedicated myself to this struggle of the African people. I have fought against white domination, and I have fought against black domination. I have cherished the ideal of a democratic and free society in which all persons live together in harmony and with equal opportunities. It is an ideal which I hope to live for and achieve. But if needs be, it is an ideal for which I am prepared to die.

In the courtroom there was complete silence as Mandela sat down. For perhaps 30 seconds the silence continued. Then from the public gallery there came a great sigh, like the release of breath, and the crying of women.

The judge turned to Bram and said, almost gently: 'You may call your next witness.' Bram called Walter Sisulu.

Sisulu was the key witness for the defence. His knowledge of the ANC and Umkhonto was greater than anyone else's. Upon him lay the burden of convincing the judge that Operation Mayibuye had been considered as a plan of action but not adopted as a policy, the issue which Bram believed was the 'hairline' around which the prospect of a death sentence revolved.

Bram led Sisulu's evidence, taking him through his political career, the history of the ANC, and the formation of Umkhonto. Sisulu explained how he had been present when Operation Mayibuye had first been placed before the high command as a plan for consideration. The implications of launching guerrilla warfare were so far-reaching that the high command had sought the views of the ANC and other organisations. Members of the high command themselves were deeply divided. There had been strong argument against the plan. Several meetings had been held to discuss it further. The last meeting had adjourned without taking a decision. 'My view,' said Sisulu, 'was that conditions did not exist at that time for Operation Mayibuye.'

Having led him through his evidence, Bram asked: 'Looking back on it, Mr Sisulu, do you consider that you could or should have acted otherwise than you did?' Sisulu replied: 'I can't see how I could have done otherwise, other than what I have done. Because even if I myself did not play the role I did, others would have done what I have done instead.'

On 20 May, Yutar began his closing address, reading through three volumes containing a summary of evidence presented to the court, attacking the accused for their politics and throwing in allegations of murder even though no such charges had been brought against the accused. But when he repeated his assertion that not only had guerrilla warfare been agreed upon but that a date had actually been set, De Wet intervened: 'Mr Yutar,' he said, 'you do concede that you failed to prove guerrilla warfare was ever decided upon, do you not?'

Yutar looked stunned. Preparations were being made, he stammered.

'Yes, I know that,' De Wet replied testily. 'The defence concedes that. What they say is that preparations were made in case one day they found it necessary to resort to guerrilla warfare. But they say prior to their arrest they never considered it necessary, and took no decision to engage in guerrilla warfare. I take it that you have no evidence contradicting that, and that you accept it?'

In a strangled voice, Yutar replied: 'As your Lordship pleases.'

In his closing address, Bram had to deal with the two most serious contentions in the case: first, that the high command had decided to embark upon guerrilla warfare; and second, that Umkhonto was the military wing of the ANC. Bram had spent weeks preparing his submissions on these points with painstaking attention to detail, but no sooner had he stated the argument he would present on the first point than De Wet cut him short, saying: 'I thought I made my attitude clear. I accept no decision or date was fixed upon for guerrilla warfare.' When Bram moved on to the second issue, De Wet again intervened, saying he accepted that though the two organisations overlapped, they were in fact separate. 'Bram's months of meticulous preparation had come to nothing, but he sat down very grateful indeed that he had not had to argue the case that he had prepared,' said Joffe. 'We were over the two worst hurdles.'

From the start of the trial, there had never been any doubt about what the verdict would be. Most of the accused freely admitted their participation in the conspiracy, though to varying degrees of involvement. The centre of interest had been on whether or not the conspirators would receive the death penalty. On 11 June 1964, Judge de Wet found all the conspirators except Bernstein guilty and reserved sentence for the following day. Bernstein was immediately surrounded by security police, hustled down to the cells, and charged with new offences.

On their way home that day, Bram and the defence team stopped at the prison to talk to the accused for the last time, and found them as resolute as ever. 'They were calm, living now in the shadow of death,' recalled Joffe. 'The strain and tension were becoming almost unbearable, yet the only matter that they wanted to discuss was how they should behave in court if the death sentence was passed. We told them that the judge would ask the first accused, Nelson Mandela: "Have you any reason to advance why the death sentence should not be passed?"'

Mandela retorted that in that case he would have a lot to say. He would tell De Wet that he was prepared to die secure in the knowledge that his death would be an inspiration to the cause of freedom. Bram pointed out that such an address would hardly help to facilitate an appeal. Mandela replied that if sentenced to death, neither he nor Sisulu nor Mbeki would appeal. They believed that an appeal would undermine the moral stand they had taken. It might be interpreted by their supporters as an act of weakness. Bram and the others left the prison dismayed by their decision.

The following morning, as Bram entered the Palace of Justice, a large crowd stood silently in the square outside, some carrying banners declaring, 'We are proud of our leaders'. Before sentence was passed, the court heard two pleas in mitigation. Though the accused had been reluctant at first to allow anyone to speak on their behalf, they eventually agreed on condition that nothing was said that could be construed as an apology. They proposed several names. A few had agreed; most declined. Joffe recalled: 'It took considerable courage at that time to stand up and speak for a group of men who had become the butt of the most tremendous barrage of hostile propaganda from the press and public platform of any accused in South African history, men who acknowledged themselves guilty of an offence which the white population of South Africa at least regarded with absolute horror.'

Bram finally gained the assistance of the author, Alan Paton. As leader of the Liberal Party, a devout believer in non-violence and a known anti-communist, Paton had often been critical of the accused, but when approached for his help he had asked one simple question:

'Are their lives in danger?' On being told yes, Paton declared: 'In that case, there is no question at all. I will give evidence if I am called.'

Paton spoke of Mandela, Sisulu and Mbeki as 'men well known for their courage, determination and ability', and told the judge that the exercise of clemency was of great importance for the future of the country. When he had finished, Yutar rose to launch an attack on Paton's character, implying that he moved readily in communist circles. As the smears continued, Paton became angry and confused. The security police witnessing the spectacle tittered.

Concluding the defence's plea in mitigation, the distinguished lawyer, Harold Hanson, whom Bram had asked to assist, spoke of how a nation's grievances could not be suppressed; how people would always find a way to give voice to those grievances. 'It was not their aims which had been criminal,' said Hanson, 'only the means to which they had resorted.' He reminded De Wet that his own Afrikaner people had conducted armed uprising, rebellion and treason in 1914, and had appeared for such offences before courts which had decided to show leniency.

De Wet appeared to be little interested in these arguments. He neither looked up nor made notes. When Hanson had finished, he nodded to the accused to rise, barely waiting for them to get to their feet, to begin his judgement.

He was not convinced, he said, that the motives of the accused were as altruistic as they claimed. 'People who organise a revolution usually take over the government, and personal ambition cannot be excluded as a motive.' The crime of which the accused had been convicted was in essence one of high treason, but the state had decided not to charge the crime in that form.

> Bearing this in mind and giving the matter very serious consideration, I have decided not to impose the supreme penalty, which in a case like this would usually be the proper penalty for the crime, but consistent with my duty that is the only leniency I can show. The sentence of all the accused will be one of life imprisonment.

De Wet had spoken so quietly that many in the public gallery had not heard the sentence. In desperation, Denis Goldberg's mother,

Annie, cried out: 'Denis! What is it?' 'Life!' he shouted back. 'Life! To live!'

As the accused were led away, down the courtroom steps to the cells below, the lawyers stood in silence, then each in turn shook hands with Bram. 'It had been his responsibility in the first place to save their lives,' remarked Joffe, 'and it was his victory in the first place that they would live.'

CHAPTER 10

DARK TIMES

On the day after the Rivonia Trial ended, Bram and Molly set out by car for Cape Town on a short holiday. They planned to arrive in Cape Town in good time to join Ilse, a student at the university there, in celebrating her twenty-first birthday.

They left Beaumont Street at midday, taking with them a young friend, Liz Lewin, who had been helping to run the Johannesburg office of an international defence fund connected with the Rivonia Trial. Bram was exhausted after all the tensions of the trial, and rested in the back of the Mercedes-Benz while Molly drove. As dusk began to fall, they changed places.

Approaching a bridge over the Sand River, south of Ventersburg in the Orange Free State, Bram saw a cow crossing the road. Coming towards them at the same time was a motorcycle. Startled by the motorcycle, the cow moved back into the path of the car. Bram veered off the road down an incline towards the river. The car came to rest on the bank, perched perilously above a deep pool of water. Bram and Liz Lewin managed to scramble out of the front windows and struggled to help Molly in the back. But she was trapped, and the car suddenly pitched forward into 30 feet of water. Frantically, Bram dived into the pool again and again, trying to reach her. But it was too late.

Bram never recovered from the death of Molly. It was to grieve him for the rest of his life. He was wracked by guilt, blaming himself for the accident. There were times when he would break down and weep. But mostly he bore the loss outwardly with fortitude and self-control, showing far more concern for others devastated by her death than for himself, concealing his own deep emotions. He also retained an extraordinary presence of mind. On arriving at the hospital in Winburg, one of his first thoughts was to ask Liz Lewin to safeguard a diary he had brought from Beaumont Street. He later asked his brother, Paul, to retrieve from the car's luggage a box of tissues that contained a map.

Returning to Johannesburg, Bram broke the news to his son, Paul, and phoned Ivan Schermbrucker. Ignoring his banning order, Schermbrucker immediately went to Beaumont Street; so did Eli Weinberg. Early in the morning, Schermbrucker went on to tell the Bernsteins and sat on their bed, sobbing. At Beaumont Street, a stream of visitors arrived, friends from the Indian and African communities sitting silently in respect. Ilse came from Cape Town, Ruth from London. In moments of distraction, Bram wandered about the house saying, '*My arme vrou*' – 'My poor wife'.

Molly was cremated one week after the end of the Rivonia Trial. Bram had asked Hilda Bernstein to speak in the chapel, but because she was subject to a banning order her words had to be read by Vernon Berrangé. About 300 people, of all races and colours and from all walks of life, attended the funeral. When it was over, as many of them were under banning orders, they quickly dispersed. 'Molly's death,' recorded Hilda Bernstein, 'is like a terrible symbol of the dark times that now lie ahead.'

In a letter to Tilly First, Ruth First's mother, which Bram wrote at this time, he revealed how important he believed the cause to be, even at a moment of such distress. 'During the past 20 years,' he wrote, 'we have had to make many important decisions which might have had grave consequences for ourselves and our family. I know that there was no single occasion when Molly ever let herself be influenced in any way by possible personal consequences. She had the rare quality, supposed to belong to judges, of being able to exclude entirely from her mind what the consequences of a decision might be to her – and what was perhaps even more remarkable – what such consequences might be to her family.'

Here there was nothing of the personal warmth for which Bram was so often noted, only a steely determination that the fight still had to be fought. The conviction that what mattered most was the cause drove Bram onwards in the coming months, relentlessly.

'From the time that Molly died, I felt that he would have given his life in any way,' remarked Hilda Bernstein. 'He became quite reckless.'

Yet she remained willing to help him, even though the cause seemed desperate. 'I felt bound to him by loyalty and love, so I did things which I didn't really want to do.' Rusty Bernstein, who had been released on bail at this time, recalled: 'After Molly died, Bram wasn't rational any more. He was driven to an excessive point. He took incredible risks. He didn't care any more. His judgement was impaired. He went over the brink.'

The day after the funeral, Bram flew to Cape Town with Joel Joffe and took the ferry to Robben Island to consult the Rivonia prisoners on the question of an appeal. When the prisoners were brought into the visitors' room, Sisulu greeted Bram and, not having heard the news, asked him about Molly, for whom he had a deep affection. Bram replied: 'Walter, Mo – Molly is all right … Molly is all right,' but his manner suggested something was wrong. Towards the end of the meeting, Mandela asked him about Molly. Bram stood up, turned away and abruptly walked from the room. He returned composed a few minutes later and resumed the conversation, but without answering Mandela's question. When the prisoners were being taken back to their cells, a prison warder explained the reasons for Bram's conduct and how Molly had died. 'We were devastated by the news,' said Mandela. 'Molly was a wonderful woman, generous and unselfish, utterly without prejudice. She had supported Bram in more ways than it was possible to know.' Mandela wrote a letter of condolence to Bram, but the prison authorities never sent it to him.

When Bram later went to see Denis Goldberg in Pretoria prison, Goldberg, having heard the news, told Bram how sorry he was about Molly. Bram clenched his fists until the knuckles turned white and carried on with the consultation.

To help ease the shock, Bram arranged a family trip to the Cape with Ruth, Ilse and Paul. They took with them a close friend of Ilse, Sholto Cross, a former student at Cape Town University who had joined the Communist Party in 1963. After spending a week in Cape Town, they stayed at a beach house near Hermanus with two old communist friends, Jack and Ray Simons, aware that the security police were keeping them under surveillance. They left on 3 July, travelling along the Garden Route, revisiting many of the places where Bram, Molly and the children had spent holidays.

As they drove through George, they were stopped by police. Though Bram knew he was being watched, he was rash enough to be carrying a number of incriminating documents. To allay suspicion, he courteously volunteered to drive to the police station, and on the way passed papers to Ruth and Ilse, telling them to hide them under their clothes. When they reached the police station, Bram pointed out how tired and hungry the girls were and suggested the police should allow them to go to a nearby restaurant while they searched the car. The girls managed to dispose of all the material in the restaurant's toilet. But one piece of paper left in the car was discovered during the search: it was a plan of how to make a bomb. The police, however, took no action and allowed Bram to go on his way.

On the way back to Johannesburg, while passing through Welkom in the Orange Free State, there was another blow. Stopping to buy a Sunday newspaper, Bram and Sholto Cross were shaken to discover that Lionel Gay, a senior figure in the new Umkhonto high command, had been arrested. When they returned home on 8 July, security police were waiting in Beaumont Street, seemingly ready to pounce. Inside the house they found Alan Brooks, a member of the small African Resistance Movement whom both Ilse and Cross knew well, on the run from Cape Town where security police had smashed the organisation. They quickly made a plan to smuggle him out of the house.

Knowing that his arrest must be imminent, Bram at once began to dispose of papers. At dawn the next morning the security police raided Beaumont Street, searching the house for four hours. Bram was arrested under the 90-day detention law, and taken first to security police headquarters at the Grays and then to his rooms at Innes Chambers, which were also thoroughly searched. He spent the night at Marshall Square police station where David Kitson was also being held. On his second day there, Sholto Cross was brought in and remained in detention for the next five months.

Bram's arrest, coming so soon after the Rivonia Trial, prompted protests in Britain and in Europe. At the Grays, the security police seemed less interested in questioning Bram than in telling him that they knew everything. Lionel Gay had begun to talk, leading them to Wilton Mkwayi and Kitson. In a stroke, the new Umkhonto high command had been wiped out. Bram too was compromised.

Late at night on 11 July, after holding him for three days, the security police released Bram, perhaps hoping that he would flee the country and rid them of the need to put him on trial. He was delivered back to Beaumont Street at midnight, just as Ruth and Ilse were going to bed, but he remained undaunted and as determined as ever to continue the fight.

Yet the underground movement he led was in tatters. Scores of activists and suspects had been detained. Some, like Lionel Gay, had readily collaborated with the security police to save themselves. Others wondered how long it would be before they too were taken. Even the Bernsteins doubted the value of trying to hold out.

'Everything was crumbling, dissolving, perishing,' wrote Hilda Bernstein in her account of these times. 'There was really no longer a veneer of ordinary living spread over the holes. We were no longer part of any community, no longer in possession of any pattern for co-operation with others, not even able to maintain a proper way of working for ourselves. We had no more discipline imposed on us by jobs and work; the only regularity was Rusty's daily reporting to the police at Marshall Square, our only discipline the necessity to observe house arrest rules. We had become not only outcasts but a danger to those left, to what we valued most.'

She recorded a conversation she had with Ivan Schermbrucker at this time. Though both were banned, they met in the evening, in the open.

'You know you are going to be arrested soon,' I told him. 'It's only a matter of days.' By that time we could see there was a pattern that made his arrest, like mine, inevitable.

He said: 'I know.'

'Then what are you going to do?'

'Nothing.'

'Just sit and wait for them to come?'

He looked at me with infinitely sad eyes. He said: 'Hilda, I can't go. How can I go? I can't bloody well go! I can't run away and leave L and M and N stuck in under 90 days. I can't go and leave Helen shut up for five years alone in her house. I can't leave Mary sitting in that square mile of Orange Grove. I can't go.'

'Then you are going to jail.'

'Yes.'

I said: 'It might be for a long time, Ivan.'

'I know. I can't go.'

And already there is a rift between us, because I am thinking of going and he is not.

One by one, the remnants of the Communist Party were hunted down. Ivan Schermbrucker, Piet Beyleveld, Esther Barsel, Jean Middleton and many other comrades of Bram were arrested. The Bernsteins managed to escape out of the back door of their house in Observatory a minute before security police arrived. With the help of Ivan Schermbrucker's wife, Lesley, and other supporters still at large, they were spirited across the border into Bechuanaland. Bram was upset at their going, still believing, like Schermbrucker, that the only proper course was to stay, whatever the cost. 'When the time came to go,' recalled Hilda Bernstein, 'I felt I was betraying Bram but not the movement. Bram though had an implacable attitude towards people who left. He believed that staying was an important demonstration, an important political act.'

But the cost for those determined to stay was indeed high, as Ivan Schermbrucker found. Under interrogation, detainees who refused to co-operate were often subjected to what was known as 'statue' torture, being forced to stand in a small chalk circle for hours on end. If they tried to sit, they were jerked to their feet; and if they fainted or lost consciousness, they were revived and forced to stand again. In a note smuggled out of prison, Schermbrucker, a strong and vigorous man, described how he was made to stand until exhaustion brought him to the ground after 28 hours. 'I fell twice, had cold water thrown over me and was pulled to my feet ... I nearly committed bloody suicide by jumping out of the window. This is torture ... They threatened to keep me standing for four days and nights and even longer.' Some detainees did commit suicide; some were tortured to death.

In the final act of the sabotage era, on 24 July, one of the few remaining activists still at large, John Harris, a Liberal Party member connected to the African Resistance Movement, filled a suitcase with explosives and a detonator and left it with an elderly woman in the white section of a Johannesburg's main railway station. It exploded, killing the woman, maiming a child and injuring a score of other whites. Harris was subsequently hanged for murder, the only white saboteur to be executed in South Africa during the apartheid era. More than any other episode, the bombing was used by the government to assert the evil nature of all anti-apartheid opponents. Bram was appalled by the futility of such violence.

Amid the collapse, Bram tried to appear optimistic and encouraging, but often seemed distracted. 'After Molly died, he didn't have much of a will to live outside that small world,' said Pat Davidson, who moved back to Beaumont Street to take care of the house once Ilse had returned to university in Cape Town and Ruth had flown back to London. 'He cried a good deal. He was a shadow of his former self.' With visitors, he would talk and laugh, then suddenly get up and leave the room to be alone. When he went to a jeweller's shop to collect an alarm clock for Ilse, an exact replica of the one he and Molly had bought as a present for her twenty-first birthday and which had been lost in the car accident, he broke down weeping.

His services as a lawyer were meanwhile still sought. He was retained to appear before the Privy Council in London in October to argue a complex case concerning patent rights in which he had been involved for several years. When he first applied for a passport to travel to London the government refused, whereupon his client, an American firm, appealed to the United States ambassador in South Africa to intervene. On 21 September, the government agreed to issue Bram with a passport.

Two days later, while Bram was working in Innes Chambers, the security police came for him again. This time they arrested him not under the 90-day detention law but under the *Suppression of Communism Act*. On 24 September, along with 13 other whites, he appeared in the Johannesburg magistrate's court accused of being a member of the illegal Communist Party. Among his fellow accused were Ivan Schermbrucker, Eli Weinberg, Esther Barsel and Jean Middleton. Missing from the line-up was one other friend who had been detained: Piet Beyleveld.

Bram immediately applied for bail, explaining to the magistrate that, despite his arrest, his American client still wanted him to appear

110

before the Privy Council. Once the hearing in London was over, he said, he had every intention of returning to South Africa in time to face trial, which was not due to begin until November. He spoke of his family history going back to the eighteenth century, of the distinguished posts held by his father and grandfather, of his long membership of the Johannesburg Bar.

'I have been interfered with by the security police for the past 14 to 15 years. I know they would like to prosecute me because of my political ideas. My home has been watched, my telephone conversations tapped, and my home and offices raided many times. I was held for three days under the 90-day clause recently. I have a tourist passport to Rhodesia, and although I am fully aware that I am being watched by the police, I have never yet tried to leave the country.'

His position was clear: 'I have no intention of avoiding a political prosecution. I fully believe I can establish my innocence. I am an Afrikaner. My home is South Africa. I will not leave South Africa because my political beliefs conflict with those of the government.'

Giving evidence on Bram's behalf, Peter Rissik, a Johannesburg attorney who was involved in the patent case, said he had known Bram for 20 years. 'I have absolute faith in his integrity. I would accept his word unhesitatingly, confident that he would carry it out.' Harold Hanson suggested that Bram's colleagues would be prepared to pay whatever amount was required for bail.

The prosecutor opposed bail. Reading from a police affidavit, he told the court that Bram was a member of the Communist Party's central committee and pointed out that many communists had fled South Africa, some of them to avoid prosecution, citing as examples Bernstein, Goldreich and Wolpe.

The magistrate, however, after a day's deliberation, disagreed. He referred to Bram as 'a son of our soil and an advocate of standing in this country'. It would be absurd, he said, for the court to prevent Bram from attending the Privy Council hearing by refusing him bail if the government had just agreed to provide him with a passport to enable him to go there.

Watching the proceedings was a young, serious-minded relative of Bram named Mollie Anderson, the daughter of a cousin, with whom Bram had corresponded. As a child, she had once seen Bram tip his hat to an African woman, a maid, and observed how the woman had drawn herself up with pride and pleasure at the gesture. After joining one of Jean Middleton's volunteer groups, she had been arrested in 1963 for distributing pamphlets, and sentenced to six months' imprisonment. During the swoop on Communist Party members in July, she had laid low. Assuming she was now safe from arrest, she ventured to court to see her friends. But a security policeman spotted her and she was arrested and charged along with the others.

A week later, Bram left for London. The government made no further attempt to impede his departure, wanting to avoid any adverse publicity and perhaps hoping that he would remain in exile, which would rid them of the need to put him on trial and discredit him at the same time.

Bram found the experience 'all a bit queer and unrealistic', he said in a letter to Ilse and Paul. He stayed at first at Grosvenor House, a Park Lane hotel, describing its air of genteel decay and coffee 'not wholly unlike the stuff at Marshall Square'. He then moved in with Ruth and Anthony Eastwood and was soon engulfed in meeting old friends and comrades from South Africa, making contact with British politicians and journalists, and preparing his case before the Privy Council. The proceedings began in the office of the Judicial Committee in Whitehall on 15 October and were adjourned for the weekend. Bram, Ruth and Anthony took advantage of the break to take a trip to Wales. On 19 October, back at the Privy Council, Bram won his case.

Bram still had two weeks left in England before he was due to return to South Africa. Many of his old comrades urged him to remain in England. Sitting on a park bench, Joe Slovo, Michael Harmel, Yusuf Dadoo and other prominent colleagues argued for hours trying to persuade him not to go back. 'We tried desperately to get him to stay outside, to break his bail conditions,' recalled Slovo.

But though he listened to their opinions, Bram had little doubt about what he should do. He had always been highly critical of those who had decided to flee South Africa. He had, moreover, given an undertaking before a court of law that he would go back. Asked by one questioner, 'Why go back?' Bram replied simply: 'Because I said I would.' But it was more than a matter of personal honour and integrity that drove him. Bram believed that his return to South Africa could be put to good use in reconstructing underground resistance. It was his mission.

Bram returned to Johannesburg on 2 November, and two weeks later duly appeared in court. The first state witness was Piet Beyleveld. Bram had known he had been co-operating with the security police but believed until the last moment that he could be persuaded not to testify in court. He sent a series of messages to Beyleveld through his wife, who had regular access to him in detention, urging him to reconsider. In London, Bram had told the South African writer, Mary Benson: 'He is one of my oldest friends, an Afrikaner like me. For eight years we were comrades together. I do not believe that when he comes into court, when he looks me in the eyes, that he will be able to give evidence against us.'

But Beyleveld did come into court and did give evidence. Jean Middleton recalled: 'The accused sat appalled at this betrayal by someone we had trusted. In the Congress of Democrats, on committees and in the unit, we had liked and respected him as a chairperson. To some of us, he had been a friend. We looked straight into his face throughout that day and a half, trying to stare him down and shame him. He remained calm and firm-voiced, and didn't seem afraid of throwing an occasional glance in our direction. His eyes had the distant, unfocused stare of someone who has been in solitary, so he didn't meet our eyes directly, but he didn't avoid them either.'

Beyleveld testified that he, together with Bram, Ivan Scherm-brucker, Eli Weinberg and Hilda Bernstein, had been members of the central committee since August 1963. He gave details of other party committees on which he had served, and identified their members. He described how the party functioned underground and how it handled finances. He discussed party documents and policies. When the prosecutor read out a passage from the Communist Party's programme and asked whether he had agreed with it, he replied: 'Yes. I still do.'

Asked by Vernon Berrangé, for the defence, why he was giving evidence, he said he had agreed after persistent questioning; he had not been ill-treated; he had been questioned for only six or seven hours; and no undue pressure had been exerted on him. When Berrangé questioned him on the ease with which he had made his statement, Beyleveld replied: 'I recognised the party had suffered complete defeat ... The shock to me was that the police knew as much as they did.'

Then Harold Hanson, who was representing Bram, questioned him about Bram. Beyleveld readily agreed that Bram was 'very widely respected in all parts of the country'; he was well known as 'the champion of the poorer people and the underprivileged classes, much concerned about their advancement'; his personal advice was sought by all kinds of men.

Hanson remarked: 'He has been widely revered?'

'Yes, and by me too,' replied Beyleveld. 'He still is.'

'I was interested to hear you say that,' said Hanson. 'I don't like to put this in my client's presence, but he is a man who carries something of an aura of a saint-like quality, does he not?'

Beyleveld replied: 'I agree.'

Thus did Beyleveld betray Bram and many other friends. For a number of them – Schermbrucker, Eli Weinberg, Esther Barsel and Norman Levy – it was Beyleveld's evidence alone that convicted them; no other evidence incriminating them was produced. In return for his testimony, he was given indemnity from prosecution and released, to be produced later as a witness at other trials. Explaining his action, he said: 'I wanted to be released from the 90-day detention. My liberty became very important to me. I can think of nothing but my liberty and I am prepared to forsake my life-long principles for it. I have no other principle but to obtain my own liberty.'

The next witness was Gerard Ludi. He introduced himself as a warrant officer in the security police, who had been recruited while he was a student to infiltrate left-wing organisations. He described his progress through the Congress of Democrats, through youth movements and discussion groups, until in May 1963 he succeeded in infiltrating the party. He went on to give details of all the meetings he had attended, including his encounters with Bram in Jean Middleton's flat. Over the years, he said, he had filed five or six hundred reports for the security police.

Bram now knew that the verdict in the trial was inevitable. But rather than wait for the outcome, he embarked upon one final act of defiance.

CHAPTER 11

INTO THE UNDERGROUND

Bram's plan was to set up from underground a new network of resistance. His difficulties were immense. Nothing in his life had prepared him for an underground existence. He needed an effective disguise and a new identity. The old network on which he had previously relied had been virtually destroyed. Only a handful of faithful friends remained.

He turned for help to his young architect friend, John Bizzell. Bizzell had already had one nasty brush with the security police. He had been part of a study group with Lionel Gay, the senior Umkhonto member who had since defected, and had once helped Gay purchase radio equipment for experiments with remote-controlled detonation. He was also a link in a chain involving a gun. Just before Ronnie Kasrils fled South Africa, he had handed Bizzell his gun. Bizzell asked Bram what he should do with it. Bram had told him to pass it on to Gay. Detained by the security police in August, Bizzell learned that they knew about the gun.

Released from detention after three weeks, Bizzell continued to run risky operations at Bram's behest. When Lionel Gay was released from detention, having given evidence in court against David Kitson and several other colleagues, Bram used Bizzell as a messenger to urge Gay not to give evidence in any further trials. Bizzell offered to help Gay escape, and Bram subsequently promised him safe passage along ANC routes, despite his betrayal. Given a compass, bus schedules and instructions about crossing points into Bechuanaland by Bizzell, Gay fled the country.

Bizzell's next task was to help furnish Bram with an underground disguise. Bizzell had previously been critical of the amateurish fashion in which activists like the Rivonia conspirators had attempted to disguise themselves. By chance, his wife, Maggie, a teacher at an exclusive girls' school in Johannesburg, was friendly with another teacher there, Diane Schoop, whose husband, Raymond, a German-born theatre designer, had sometimes referred to his family's experiences of life underground during the Nazi era. As a youth in Hamburg, he had listened to many accounts of the clandestine activities of anti-Nazis in Hamburg, and had acquired an acute understanding of what was required to survive underground. He had since settled in South Africa, working for the National Theatre in Pretoria. He had played no part in any political activity and was consequently unknown to the security police, but Bizzell knew that he possessed left-wing sympathies.

Bizzell at first approached Schoop for advice in general about disguises, but later confided in him that it was Bram Fischer who wanted help. Schoop knew little about Bram other than what he had read in newspapers, but agreed to meet him briefly at a hotel in a Johannesburg suburb to make sure he had the right potential.

Bram also involved close friends who were still at large. All were known to the security police, and all faced considerable risk. Violet Weinberg, whose husband was one of the communists on trial with Bram, said she thought his plan was crazy. If Bram stood trial he would serve a limited sentence; if he went underground and was recaptured, the result would be far worse. But such was the loyalty that Bram inspired among his friends that she agreed to help.

Another friend to whom he turned was Lesley Schermbrucker, Ivan's wife. She and Ivan had known the Fischers for 20 years. Though Lesley had never been as politically active as Violet Weinberg, she too agreed to help. Bram also approached Ralph and Mini Sepel. Despite their low profile, they had been caught up in the Rivonia net as a result of Ralph Sepel's legal work on the purchase of Lilliesleaf. In 1963 he had been detained for five weeks. But otherwise the Sepels were considered relatively safe.

As well as establishing a support group for himself, Bram endeavoured to reconstruct a new central committee. Both Violet and Lesley were inducted as members, together with Issy Heymann, an old communist stalwart whose career had included everything from concession store-keeper to watchmaker to bicycle shop manager. But the new members merely served to underline how few of the party faithful were left.

At Beaumont Street, Bram made what preparations he could for his family. In December, Ilse completed her degree at Cape Town University and returned to Johannesburg, intending to take up articles with a law firm. Because of the Fischer connection, one firm after another turned her down before she managed to find a position. Ilse too became part of Bram's support group and a member of the central committee. Her friend, Sholto Cross, released from prison after five months' detention and working as a journalist, also joined the support group. Paul meanwhile had managed to cope with the family up-heavals undaunted, taking care of his own medical needs and gaining distinction in his final-year examinations at school. The plan for Paul was for him to leave for London where he would stay with Ruth and Anthony Eastwood.

With the coming of the summer rains, Beaumont Street seemed just as ever like an idyllic haven. 'The garden, of course, has been perfect,' Bram wrote to a friend in London. 'The roses and petunias are lovely, summer flowers are just starting and I'm finding all sorts of queer little plants Molly must have discovered and brought in. The garden is a real monument to her this year.'

During the Christmas recess Mary Benson, the South African writer based in London, who had once worked for the treason trial defence fund, arrived in Johannesburg. 'It's like the coming of a whole battalion,' Bram welcomed her with delight. She lunched at Beaumont Street, a convivial family occasion laid out under the spreading tree by the swimming pool. Ilse and Paul were there, and Sholto Cross and Pat Davidson and the Berrangés. As he surveyed the garden, Bram remarked: 'Never has there been a lovelier summer.'

When the trial resumed in January, Mary Benson suggested to Bram that he should write an article about the crisis in South Africa for publication in the London *Observer* at the end of the trial. Bram agreed to do so, and on a Friday afternoon, 22 January, he handed her the article in a coffee bar for her to send to London. Gripping her hand, he said: 'I want you to be in court on Monday.'

Among the letters that Bram wrote when he returned to Beaumont Street was one for Mary Benson.

Dear, dear Mary,

I feel incredibly dishonest and have been ever since our talk on Friday. This is so not because I am about to 'jump' my bail. The other side has never played according to the rules and has changed the rules whenever it has suited them. That is the least of my 'moral' worries. But throughout our talk on Friday I had to act to you and pretend I would see you on Monday and that was a singularly unpleasant experience. It was made far worse by the idea which kept asserting itself that you will think on Monday when you hear I have gone, that I did not trust you. Please believe that is not so. Throughout my somewhat slender preparations for leaving I have not allowed anyone in or near the family to know of my plans and I dared not let you run the risk of having been placed, even remotely, in the position of an accessory ...

It is very early in the morning and a glow is touching the garden that Molly and I tended for more than 25 years. I have wondered and wondered what she would have advised in the present circumstances. I think she would have approved.

In some ways I suppose this would seem to be a crazy decision. Yet I feel it is up to someone among the whites in Johannesburg to demonstrate a spirit of real revolt. Until we have something like that, we shall drift on and on into chaos and our self-destruction. It must be demonstrated that people can fight apartheid from within the country even though it may be dangerous. That is why I returned here. I have left the trial because I also want to demonstrate that no one should meekly submit to our barbaric laws ...

I'm sure we shall meet again.

Love Bram

He also wrote two letters to Ilse, one of them intended for the benefit of the security police.

Ilse my darling,

I wish I could be with you when you open this – just to steady you a bit when you find out I've left home and am going to try and carry on my political work in hiding.

Apart from the difficulty of making the decision to leave the accused and possibly be accused myself of running away, I have been haunted by the idea of leaving you with everything to handle – the house, chambers, etc. – and doing so without even saying goodbye.

But it could not have been otherwise. This was the one occasion on which I simply could not consult you about a major decision.

So this will have to be my goodbye to you. I have written some details to Pat and have enclosed in her envelope a copy of a letter I am sending to Harold [Hanson]. That will explain something of what I feel.

Hold thumbs for me as I shall hold mine for you. Don't worry. We shall be again together in happier times.
All my love,
Bram

The other letter, marked strictly private and confidential, was more personal.

I've written you a note – a bit formal – because it may fall into the hands of the police. Even this may, but you can read it and tear it up if you wish ...

He spoke of how their hearts would break when they came to leave Beaumont Street.

Ours has been a lovely home with a beautiful garden. Many, many years ago when old man Hutton and I used to catch the bus together, he said to me that our garden would one day become a showpiece, and that came true. But to me the garden and home have always been much more than a showpiece. They have been a sort of epitome of all that Molly was and what she stood for: Friendliness and warmth, strength and love. God, what a terrible thing I did when I had that accident. At times I could nearly go mad with remorse and despair ...

I supposed if you look at it as a whole one should not allow oneself to be broken by a death. Death must come, sooner or later. The vital thing is that it should not be drawn out, with suffering.

Therefore one must turn to life and away from death, however deeply one loved the dead. Of the past we must think only of the magnificent years we had with Molly, despite all our tribulations. It was a life that was real and glowing.

Shortly afterwards Ilse drove Bram, crouching low in the back of his Volkswagen, to Killarney. She then returned to Beaumont Street where she and Pat Davidson did their best to create the impression that Bram was still there, asking the Fischers' faithful servant, Tias, to cook supper for three and loudly calling for Bram to come and eat when it was ready. Before going to bed, Ilse put on Bram's pyjamas and went round the house parting the curtains and checking the windows, just as Bram habitually did. The next day, Harold Hanson called round to collect the letter Bram had written that he was due to read out in court the following day. There was panic for a moment when Pat Davidson forgot where she had hidden it.

The plan worked, giving Bram a vital two-day head start over the security police. Newspapers reporting the nation-wide hunt for him carried graphic accounts of how Bram had sneaked out of his house while Ilse and Pat Davidson were asleep. Readers were told that only when the girls had realised that Bram would be late for court had they knocked on his bedroom door, to find the room empty except for a pile of letters by the bedside addressed to friends and legal advisers.

The security police swarmed into the house, turning it over, and discovered a document about bomb-making with notations in Bram's handwriting, the original of a photocopy in their possession which they had been searching for since the Rivonia Trial. They returned once more to dig up a flower bed the day after Ilse and Pat, having a quiet drink one evening and knowing that their conversations were monitored through bugging devices, had joked that the flowers at the bottom of the garden appeared to be moving, which meant that it was time to go and feed Bram.

In London, *The Observer* published extracts from the article Bram had written under the heading: 'Word from missing QC'. Bram's message was a warning of dangers ahead:

In 1965 South Africa presents a surface of ebullient confidence: the ebullience of a white electorate basking in phenomenal prosperity; and the confidence of a government which, during 16 years, has with increasing violence attempted to crush every effort by the majority of the people to win human rights until today it appears supremely stable ...

The state thinks it has crushed the liberation movement, but it has not. As we know from history – including the history of South Africa – if the struggle for freedom is smothered in one place or for the time being, it flares up again before long. In 1960, with the mass arrests during the Emergency, it seemed as if the struggle had been crushed. But this was not so. There was a resurgence in the movement for liberation.

Now of course the set-back has been more profound and widespread. But the struggle will surge forward again. It is in this that the real danger lies.

If South Africans have to perform the task by themselves, they will inevitably be driven by the terrorist methods of the state into a violent and chaotic form of struggle. And the more prolonged the daily, incessant humiliation meted out by the majority of whites, to the millions of non-whites, the fiercer the bitterness being created in millions of souls.

He went on:

A peaceful transition can be brought about if the government agrees to negotiation with all sections of the people, and, in particular, with the non-white leaders at present gaoled on Robben Island or in exile. Prospects of such negotiation seem desperately remote. The government presents a 'granite' attitude. Not one of the three prime ministers produced by the Nationalist Party since 1948 even met or talked with a single non-white leader.

Yet this is no static situation ... If the combination of predictable and unpredictable forces leads to large-scale violence or war, the consequences would be so disastrous in loss of life, in suffering, in economic disruption, in a legacy of bitter hatred and in the threat to world peace, that I believe that white South

Africans must at some stage be brought to realise that their own long-term interests lie not in maintaining race supremacy but in extending human rights to all.

When copies of *The Observer* appeared for sale in Johannesburg, the article had been excised.

At Beaumont Street, Ilse began the disheartening task of packing up the family home. Day by day, she collected together Bram's possessions: a paperweight bearing an orange-and-white fragment of the last flag flown by the independent Free State; letters his grandfather had written trying to mediate between Kruger and Milner; family letters from the Anglo-Boer War; letters of his romance with Molly; ancient press cuttings; law books and legal papers; and the note that Ouma Steyn had written to Bram on his twenty-first birthday: 'As a child and as a student you were an example to everyone. I know that you are going to play an honourable role in the history of South Africa.'

Once she received what appeared to be a coded message from Bram referring to the car and 'pink heels'. Believing it to be of vital importance, Ilse went through the Volkswagen with a fine-tooth comb, before realising that all Bram meant was the view he had had of her barefoot heels working the pedals while he was crouching low in the back of the car on the day of his escape. But she heard no other news from him.

CHAPTER 12

THE FUGITIVE

From his rendezvous in Killarney, Bram was driven by Bizzell to a small colony of theatre people in Kilnerton on the outskirts of Pretoria where Schoop lived. For the next few days, while the hue and cry over his disappearance spread across South Africa, he remained hidden in Schoop's house. The following weekend Schoop drove him in a minibus belonging to the Performing Arts Council of the Transvaal to a cottage on a remote citrus farm in the Magaliesberg district. It was here that Schoop began work on Bram's new identity.

Bram was immediately put on a spare diet. His portly frame began to shrink; his ruddy face appeared less florid. The thick grey hair on his head was shaved back to give him a receding hairline, and what was left was dyed auburn. He grew a goatee beard, which made him look like Lenin, and took to smoking a pipe, which altered the quality of his voice. His familiar black-rimmed spectacles were replaced with light-rimmed ones. He spent hours practising a different style of walking, changing the rolling gait he had habitually used since his rugby injury at Oxford to shorter, quicker steps, by walking on his heels.

As well as working on Bram's physical appearance, Schoop insisted that he should develop a distinctive new character. The key to survival, he believed, was not for Bram to fade as inconspicuously as possible into the background, but for him to emerge as a new person, with a different profession, a different family background, different habits, tastes and mannerisms. Schoop bought an entirely new wardrobe, choosing colours and styles that Bram never usually wore. The plan was for Bram to become a professional photographer, carrying camera bags over his shoulder that would make him easily recognisable. The new name he chose was an English one, Douglas Black.

For week after week Bram rehearsed his new identity, living a hermit-like existence in his sparsely furnished cottage. His only visitors were Schoop, who drove over about twice a week to check on his progress, and an elderly lady who lived in the main farmhouse, Felicia Milindton, a former Communist Party supporter who knew of Bram's true identity. Otherwise he was left to his own devices.

The loneliness constantly preyed on him. He was unaccustomed to a solitary life, and yearned for news of his friends and family. Doubts about the wisdom of his decision surfaced again and again.

He was deeply wounded to learn that the Johannesburg Bar Council had begun proceedings in the Supreme Court to have Bram's name struck from the roll of advocates, citing his conduct as 'unbefitting that of an advocate'. He saw it not only as a betrayal by his colleagues but a spurious manoeuvre. Disbarment was a device intended specifically to protect the public against unscrupulous lawyers abusing their position for personal gain. Now it was being used as a political weapon to vilify Bram's reputation in a profession in which he had spent his whole working life, and which he still held dear.

Using Raymond Schoop as a postbox, he wrote to Harold Hanson asking him to intercede with the Bar Council and questioning their right to take such action against him. At first, he told Hanson, he had thought of ignoring the matter since it was clear the government intended to terminate his legal career anyway. But a vital principle was at stake, namely: 'Whether I am to be struck off the roll because I disagree radically with the Nationalist racial policy (and am prepared to fight for my point of view) or whether I am to be struck off, after 30 years of practice, for dishonourable conduct.'

Setting out his argument, Bram invoked a legal tradition long established in South Africa that offences committed because of an overriding belief in the moral validity of a political principle did not constitute grounds for dismissal. He cited precedents dating back to the Anglo-Boer War and the Afrikaner rebellion of 1914.

When an advocate does what I have done, his conduct is not determined by any disrespect for the law nor because he hopes personally to benefit by any 'offence' he may commit. On the contrary, it requires an act of will to overcome his deeply rooted respect of legality, and he takes the step only when he feels that, whatever the consequences to himself, his political conscience no longer permits him to do otherwise. He does it not because of a desire to be immoral, but because to act otherwise would, for him, be immoral.

His original intention had been to stand trial, he said, but during the course of the proceedings he had changed his mind because of the way in which the judicial process had been contaminated by political interference. He cited two particular reasons: firstly, no prosecution that relied on evidence extracted from witnesses subjected to extended periods of solitary confinement could be regarded as fair; secondly, he was no longer facing an independent judiciary but one that could be overridden by the government in determining the length of prison sentences.

I cannot believe that any genuine protest made against the system which has been constructed solely to further apartheid can be regarded as immoral or as justifying the disbarment of a member of our profession.

He was particularly angry at the haste with which the Bar Council's decision had been taken, and at their failure to consult him on the reasons for his action.

My contention is that if in the year 1965 I have to be removed from the roll of practising advocates, the minister and not the Bar Council should do the dirty work.

Few voices were raised in support of Bram. Harold Hanson resolutely took up his defence. A former judge of the Supreme Court, Leslie Blackwell, drew attention to other historical precedents supporting Bram's case, pointing out that the current minister of justice, John Vorster, had not been disbarred for his pro-Nazi activities during the Second World War, even though he had been held in detention. But little else was heard.

In a long letter to Ruth in London, Bram wrote:

I know what my bourgeois friends would have liked me to do: To make a nice speech at the end of my trial, explaining why I did what I did – i.e. not because I am a Marxist, but because I am a humanitarian – and then to go quietly to jail hoping that (i) my presence would diminish all sentences; (ii) I would be capable of being used in a campaign for the release of political prisoners; and (iii) if I were in jail, other prisoners would receive better treatment than they are at present.

But Bram dismissed all those arguments:

It seemed to me that this was the psychological moment for someone to try and demonstrate (i) that outside of special circumstances, you must remain in the country even if there is a charge against you; (ii) that if a white man can do it, others can do so more easily; and (iii) that there are things to be done inside the country.

He spoke optimistically about the future:

There must come a revival even though it will be very slow and have to be performed with painstaking care.

On a summer's night in March 1965, Raymond Schoop drove Bram back to Johannesburg and left him in a parking lot near Jeppe station. Bram made his way to a rendezvous at the Marymount nursing home in Kensington. In the dark, the contact he was due to meet, Ralph Sepel, at first failed to recognise him and walked by. Bram had to call after him. When they reached the Sepels' house in Mons Road in Observatory, both Ralph and Mini were astonished by the change in his appearance. He walked differently, his build was slim, his mannerisms had changed, his hair had been dyed, his accent had altered, he carried a walking stick, and his dress was more English-looking; he frequently wore sports shirts. The Sepels' children thought he resembled Professor Calculus from the *Tintin* books.

Bram stayed with the Sepels for several weeks while waiting for a rented house in Knox Street in Waverley, less than a mile away from Beaumont Street, to become available. The arrangements were made for him by a young university graduate who used the name Ann

Getcliffe but whose real name was Gabriella Veglio, and who was the daughter of a wealthy businessman who lived in Houghton. In early January, before Bram jumped bail, she had approached an estate agent in Rosebank who had advertised the house for rent, and paid him six months' rent in advance. She had also purchased for Bram a light-grey Volkswagen, paying for it in cash. She stayed at Knox Street for only a short while before leaving for Europe, explaining to the estate agent that her mother had suddenly fallen ill and that an uncle would stay at the house.

Thus did Douglas Black, professional photographer, take up residence at 57 Knox Street. He introduced himself to the neighbours and made enquiries about joining a local bowling club. Writing to Ruth of his time in the 'nursing home', as he described his Magaliesberg hideout, Bram confessed: 'I felt so terribly isolated as I had not, in a way, anticipated what it would be like day after day ... But I've got used to it now. I've made some good friends who come over and have a meal or tea with me.'

Despite the risks, Bram kept in touch with a small circle of his old friends, unable to sever the links. They referred to him as 'Max'. His most regular companions, his minders, were Violet Weinberg and Lesley Schermbrucker, both of them well known to the security police. The Sepels often invited him for meals, took him to the theatre, and acted as a safe address for correspondence. Raymond Schoop introduced him to theatre friends, commissioned him to photograph dress rehearsals he was directing, invited him to spend weekends in Pretoria, and once took him to watch a cricket match at the Wanderers.

Everywhere he went, the disguise seemed effective. Bram tested it to the limit time and again. On one occasion, he returned to his old chambers and took the lift, standing close to lawyers whom he knew well. On another occasion, he stepped into a lift with Pat Davidson at the building where she worked; all that she noticed at the time was 'a funny little man' who made some remark about the weather. John Bizzell also failed to recognise him when they first met. A security policeman coming towards him in Commissioner Street, who knew him well, showed no sign of recognition. A doctor who examined Bram for high blood pressure gave no hint he suspected anything amiss.

Yet the loneliness never left him. He hankered for closer company,

and soon arranged to meet Ilse. Waiting for him in a deserted ware-
house in an industrial area south of Johannesburg, Ilse was startled
when the door opened and a man unrecognisable to her walked in.
For a fleeting moment she feared she had fallen into a police trap,
before realising that it was Bram. Even though Ilse was at greater risk
of police surveillance than even Violet Weinberg and Lesley Schermbrucker, they continued to meet regularly about once a week. Ilse took
elaborate precautions to ensure that no one followed her, varying her
meeting places from street corners to underground car parks, but she
often risked motorbike rides with Sholto Cross and another friend,
John Kalk, both of whom were well known to the security police.
Sometimes Bram would drive past Ilse's flat, just in the hope of
catching sight of her.

Unknown to his faithful minders, Bram also began to see Pat
Davidson. At Bram's suggestion, after moving out of Beaumont
Street, she had detached herself from the Fischers' world, pursuing a
routine of boyfriends, country clubs and squash that had once been
more familiar to her. Her only contact had been a few messages and
letters passed on by Lesley Schermbrucker. One day, at her law office,
a parcel arrived for her, addressed in Bram's handwriting, containing
a beautiful vase. Then Bram arranged to meet her one evening outside the squash courts where she regularly played and drove her to
Knox Street, swearing her to complete secrecy, to avoid upsetting his
minders.

Their meetings occurred more and more frequently, sometimes two
or three times a week. Pat also phoned him usually once a day. Bram
became increasingly dependent on her company. 'He found it very
difficult being alone,' she recalled. 'He was quite the wrong person to
go underground. It was important for him to have people around. He
needed to talk to people.'

Another friend to whom Bram turned was Mary Benson. Not
knowing what was expected, she was invited one night to an urgent
meeting with Violet Weinberg and Lesley Schermbrucker. Signalling
that the room might be bugged, they communicated through notes,
using the code-name of Max. 'Max is depressed and isolated, will you
visit him?' They drew her a map of how to get to Knox Street.

The next day, wearing a scarf and heavy make-up, Mary Benson walked up the long drive at 57 Knox Street, past an unkempt garden and tennis court, and rang the doorbell. A maid answered and motioned her into a large hall furnished only with cane garden chairs and a table. When Bram appeared, auburn-bearded, with receding auburn hair, wearing rimless spectacles, it took her some moments to recognise him. 'You look like Lenin,' she remarked, embracing him.

Bram picked up a pipe. 'I've taken to smoking. It helps disguise my voice. And see how thin I've got. My walk,' he demonstrated to her, 'not so bandy-legged!' The maid brought tea.

'As we talked, I began to realise how cut off he was,' wrote Mary Benson in her autobiography. 'Clearly he desperately missed family and friends.'

She had been due to fly back to London, but decided to postpone her return. She took to visiting him once or twice a week. During the daytime, they would have lunch or tea in the garden. Bram loved to catch up on news and gossip. Then he would spend part of the day typing letters or reports and collecting clippings from the newspapers and pottering about in the garden.

Bram talked about Afrikaner history, about his love of the Afrikaans language, and about communism. He mentioned he had been reading the Bible which he used when writing letters in code. 'There's so much love in it, and goodness,' he said, 'but now only *we* are carrying on those ideas.' When Mary argued that all religions, faiths and ideologies, including communism, were eventually corrupted, Bram retorted: 'It's not a question of faith. Marxism is a science, just as biology and chemistry are.' And in exasperation, he asked: 'Can't you understand that Marxism is the solution to the world's injustice? That the future lies with socialism?' Marxists, he said, were working for a new world where everything could be scientifically worked out; therefore, man's possibilities were infinite. At times he exploded in anger when talking of communism's critics, like Arthur Koestler.

Sometimes they went for drives in the countryside, taking picnics to places Bram had visited with Molly. 'I sensed how profoundly he missed Molly,' Mary wrote. 'Yet he was a perfect host – the fire deftly made, the chops well grilled, the drinks iced. Each picnic became a festive occasion.'

On the day that the Johannesburg court was due to pass judgement on his fellow communists, Bram and Mary drove to Volksrust for a picnic. Mary noticed how in sunlight the white roots of his auburn hair were exposed, and on their return to Johannesburg they stopped at a chemist shop where she bought him the dye he used. The evening papers reported how Eli Weinberg and Ivan Schermbrucker had been sentenced to five years, the others to two years. Five years was the likely sentence Bram would have been given.

The press meanwhile continued to speculate on his whereabouts. Newspaper reports suggested variously he was disguised as a priest or an elderly invalid women swathed in shawls, or 'passing' as an Indian or living in Dar-es-Salaam or South West Africa.

Yet even though he evaded capture, Bram achieved little during these months. He managed to keep in touch with a few old-time communist colleagues but made no headway in establishing a new network of activists. Even the most stalwart party members, like Jack and Ray Simons, decided to give up and emigrate to Zambia. In a letter to Ruth, Bram described their departure as 'a very poor show' with bad effects. 'This sort of thing must stop. We cannot afford for a moment to give the impression that we are *not* on the winning side.'

Yet his own attempts at stimulating action were forlorn. When the government decided to segregate Africans attending the Rand Easter Show, Bram wanted to send out circulars urging Africans to boycott the show, but had to ask Mary Benson for help in addressing envelopes. Thinking this to be a futile gesture and knowing how many young activists had been imprisoned for such activity, she refused. He spent much time working on party documents but few people ever read them.

He remained in contact with communist exiles in London. But the London group never showed as much interest in his underground work as he had expected. He was deliberately kept short of funds, and his requests for assistance went unanswered. Though the London group promised to send out a party member to help him, no one arrived. He asked them to provide him with a passport in case he needed to take a break from South Africa, but nothing happened for months.

The main purpose of his underground existence, in fact, became to evade capture. Every day he survived he regarded as a defeat for the government. When Sholto Cross was in prison, Bram used to quote to Ilse lines from a poem by Nazim Hikmet which now became his own mantra:

It may not be a pleasure exactly
But it's your solemn duty
To live one more day
To spite the enemy.

Nelson Mandela remembered how Bram's decision to go underground had a 'tremendous impact', boosting prisoner morale. The Sepels remarked: 'For as long as Bram was not caught, it was a beacon for the movement.'

In a letter to Ruth in May 1965 explaining his determination to stay, Bram remarked: 'Somehow, I feel there's nothing else to do. You see, in some ways life ended for me last year and now there's only a job to do.' His grief over Molly's death overshadowed all else. 'A year is still too short to prevent the incessant aching void.'

Yet by relying so heavily on close friends he was endangering not only himself but them. The original plan had been to cut himself off from his old life once he had re-established himself in Johannesburg. Yet he could not bring himself to do it. When the Sepels remonstrated, urging him to stay away from Violet and Lesley and Ilse for safety's sake, he became ill-tempered, refusing to heed their advice. 'Bram had lots of courage,' said Ralph Sepel, 'but he couldn't stand being on his own.'

In mid-July, he moved from Knox Street to a rented semi-detached house in Corlett Drive, close to one of Johannesburg's busiest highways, Louis Botha Avenue. He explained to neighbours that he had come from Cape Town for health reasons. He became a regular customer at the local shops, purchasing an afternoon newspaper at the same time every day on the corner of Corlett Drive and Louis Botha Avenue. The local butcher thought he looked like 'some funny old professor'. Sometimes he was followed by a stray dog.

Like the house in Knox Street, Bram's Corlett Drive hideout was sparsely furnished. He used the same garden furniture. Books and newspapers were piled on the floor. He followed the same routine, writing letters, working on party papers, reading widely, and making occasional forays to the theatre and the opera. He studied how the underground had survived in Portugal.

He had long conversations with Mary Benson, once appealing to her to join the party. 'Come over to us, Mary! Become a part of something great, be with the people!' But Mary refused: 'Although I loved and admired him, I could not join him.' Pat Davidson took him to the Kruger National Park and on weekend trips, and there were picnics with Ilse; once Sholto Cross came too. A passport eventually arrived for him from the London group, but no other help was forthcoming. 'Bram felt betrayed by his comrades in London,' recalled Pat.

Increasingly tired of his underground existence, he considered the idea of leaving South Africa for a month to gain some rest before returning to the fray, but he took no action. He sensed his struggle was becoming increasingly futile and found the loneliness unbearable. When Pat Davidson failed to phone him one day, he became upset with her. 'Towards the end,' recalled Raymond Schoop, 'he felt useless, he felt he had come to a dead end.'

Desperately short of funds, Bram made an arrangement for Pat Davidson to leave a packet of money inside a telephone directory in a call-box on the corner of Corlett Drive and Louis Botha Avenue. Pat duly left the money there and rang Bram twice, putting down the phone each time he answered, as the signal for him to come and collect it. She went to a nearby café to watch and make sure that he found the packet, noticing a man there clearly loitering. Growing increasingly suspicious, she saw Bram enter the call-box, search for the packet, fail to find it and step outside again. At this point she made off for her car, keeping her head down, refusing even to glance in Bram's direction in case some gesture of recognition was observed. As she drove away, she caught sight of Bram back in the call-box, clutching the packet. With such nerve-wracking incidents, everyone sensed that the end was near.

The final blows came in quick succession. On 2 November, the verdict in the Bar Council's case calling for Bram to be struck off the roll of advocates was handed down by the judge-president, Quartus de Wet, the same judge who had presided over the Rivonia Trial. 'It is clear,' said De Wet, 'that Mr Fischer made full use of his status as a senior counsel in inducing the magistrate to grant bail, and his breach of the solemn assurance that he would stand his trial can clearly be stigmatised as dishonest conduct. In this respect I can see no distinction between the words dishonest and dishonourable.'

He went on: 'It is also clear from Mr Fischer's letter, and his absconding from his trial, that not only was he guilty of subversive conduct in the past, but that he intended continuing such activity.'

Accordingly, he ordered Bram's name to be struck from the roll of advocates. Two other judges concurred with the verdict.

Bram read a report of the proceedings in an afternoon newspaper. 'His anguish and anger were deeply distressing to experience,' recalled Mary Benson who met him that evening. 'As we drove along, in a torrent of words he expressed his feelings: he'd done all he could, worked terribly hard, to uphold the law, struggled for justice – and surely colleagues who'd known him for 30 years should have the sense, the feeling and the courage to understand his recent actions?'

Bram suggested they should drive to a hotel in Corlett Drive to cheer themselves up with a gin and tonic. Then they had a meal at his house and listened to music. Afterwards Bram drove Mary to a taxi rank in Hillbrow. 'How can I ever thank you?' he said. 'You've saved my sanity. Can you have supper next week?'

Six days later, the security police arrested Violet Weinberg. They had been watching her for some days, ever since a party colleague, Issy Heymann, had broken under interrogation. Heymann had no direct knowledge of Bram's whereabouts. Because he was a marked man, detained once previously in 1964, he had played no role in Bram's support group. But he had known of Violet Weinberg's involvement, information which proved to be dangerous. Held under a new detention law known as the *180-day Act*, and interrogated continuously for two days and two nights, collapsing intermittently, Heymann eventually gave up Violet's name. Back in his prison cell, in shame and despair, he tried to commit suicide by slashing his wrists and ankles with a razor blade. He was taken to hospital where, after surgery, he managed to pass a message to his wife Anne, warning her that 'comrade aunty', as he called Violet, using a Yiddish phrase, was in a bad condition and should go abroad for treatment.

Anne passed on the warning to Violet during an hour-long meeting they had in the ladies' cloakroom of John Orr's department store, a place where the security police watching Violet were unable to follow. But Violet, known for her indomitable nature, refused to go into hiding. 'I think she may have wanted to prove it was possible to withstand the pressures of detention, sleep deprivation and interrogation,' said Jean Middleton who served a prison sentence with her, 'but no one could withstand them.'

Arrested at noon at the shop where she worked, Violet was taken first to the Grays, where she managed to dispose of some letters in a toilet, and then to security police headquarters in Pretoria. For 70 hours she held out, interrogated without stop in a small, airless room, with the windows closed and shuttered against the light, standing for hour after hour, sometimes managing to sit on the floor or a radiator, and kept awake by a relay of interrogators who banged the table whenever she showed signs of sleeping. They threatened her two children and warned she would end up in a mental asylum. Once she told them: 'You are like a group of sadistic schoolboys pulling the wings of a fly, and I feel like the fly.' One of the questions they hammered away with concerned the identity of a man seen recently in her company with a goatee beard, a moustache, receding hair and thin-rimmed spectacles, whom they took to be a contact with Bram, not realising it was Bram himself. Even to the very last, Bram's disguise had worked.

Within an hour of Violet's arrest, Lesley Schermbrucker found out what had happened and telephoned to warn Bram. From all previous experience they knew that Violet would not be able to hold out for much more than 48 hours. Bram began to look for a new house to rent, and found one advertised in Dunkeld, but it was not available until mid-December and he did not have sufficient funds for a deposit. He seemed virtually paralysed by the turn of events, unable to come up with any new ideas, perhaps knowing the end was at hand. He asked Mary Benson to arrange an appointment for him with a visitor from London, Diana Collins, a prominent supporter of the anti-apartheid campaign, wanting to thank her for all her support, seemingly oblivious of the risk to both of them.

Ralph Sepel met Bram at Craighall Park Hotel on 10 November, adamant that he should not even think about returning to Corlett

Drive, but stay instead at a hotel while another plan was made. Bram agreed to do so, but still went back that night to Corlett Drive. The next day, he phoned the Sepels from a call-box, jubilant at the news of Ian Smith's declaration of independence in neighbouring Rhodesia, believing that it would swiftly lead to revolution there. 'This is *Uhuru*!' he exclaimed. When Mini Sepel asked whether he had moved from his house, he said not yet, that he had one more letter to write. In the afternoon, he watered the garden and passed the time of day with a neighbour, saying he intended to grow figs.

At about 6 pm on 11 November, shortly after driving away from his hideout in Corlett Drive, Bram was stopped by security police who had been watching the property. When a police lieutenant addressed him as Mr Fischer, Bram indignantly claimed his name was Douglas Black. But the chase was over. It had lasted for 290 days.

CHAPTER 13

FISCHER'S TRIAL

The police swoop on Bram showed how little preparation he had made to conceal his tracks. Among his possessions they found note-books; party discussion papers; letters in code; envelopes with cash; false identity papers; bank documents; false car number plates; copies of the party journal, *African Communist*; and a whole range of disguise equipment – false beards, false eyebrows, a wig, a variety of face creams, tins of 'tan-in-a-minute' lotion, mascara and face powder. There was even a complete outfit of women's clothing in Bram's size, a corset, some wool and knitting needles.

When news of his arrest broke on the radio, his few faithful minders hastily discussed what they should do. The Sepels, with two young sons, decided to leave immediately. In one frantic and tumultuous day, they applied for passports, bought air tickets, drew money from the bank, packed clothes and rushed to the airport, abandoning their house, furniture and other possessions. For Lesley Schermbrucker, the decision was harder; she also had two teenage children but knew that she could not leave South Africa with her husband in prison, even though it meant for her in all likelihood arrest and imprisonment. Ilse, fearing arrest at any moment, went into hiding.

On 15 November, Bram was taken from Pretoria Local prison to appear at the magistrate's court in Johannesburg. The courthouse bristled with security police. Bram had shaved off his beard, and above his forehead a short, grey stubble had begun to appear. Reporters noticed how much thinner he was. Among the crowd in the courtroom were Ruth and Paul, who had arrived from London.

While waiting for a preliminary hearing to begin in January 1966, Bram settled down to a prison routine of reading books and writing letters. As an awaiting-trial prisoner, his conditions were relatively comfortable. He was allowed two private visits a week, fresh clothing when he wanted it, and food kept in his cell. He had two exercise periods a day, but was otherwise locked up for 23 out of 24 hours a day.

His lawyer, George Bizos, pondering like many others why Bram had sacrificed his family life and career for an underground escapade which had seemed to achieve so little, asked him whether it had all been worth it. Bram's angry response was to ask whether Bizos had put the same question to Nelson Mandela; did not Mandela have a family life and career? Bizos admitted that he had not asked Mandela. 'Well then, don't ask me,' Bram retorted.

Pat Davidson also visited Bram regularly, using her position as Bram's attorney to act as a courier for him, smuggling letters out of prison and even taking with her a map of the prison he had drawn in case an escape plan could be organised. With her, Bram was more forthright in admitting that he had achieved little by going underground.

He meanwhile prepared his defence before the court, drawing on many of the old texts which helped sustain his belief in Marxism and his commitment to the Communist Party. 'Do you want a tonic?' he wrote to Ilse on 16 December. 'Do what I did today and study Uncle Karl's manifesto again. The political polemic in Section III is of course out of date, but for the rest – what a superb document. And what of course is fascinating is to read it as applicable to the modern world where capital is exploiting not only African peasants but an African proletariat.' He asked Ruth and Ilse to check on an inscription on the statue of Paul Kruger in Church Square in Pretoria which he wanted to use in his address to the court.

On 26 January 1966 the prosecution outlined its case against Bram, accusing him of involvement in plans to overthrow the government. Bram, said the prosecution, had participated in meetings at Rivonia to discuss sabotage and the recruitment and training of saboteurs. He had helped draft documents, handled party funds and chaired meetings of the central committee. 'At meetings he lost his temper a few times and hit the table with his fists to impress his fellow members. Not only did he approve of sabotage, but he gave his active support in the form of suggestions and by making money available for the work of Umkhonto.' In the post-Rivonia era, said the prosecution, Bram was 'like an army general who after a shattering defeat tries to reorganise the scattered remnants of his army'.

A steady stream of witnesses was called. The elderly retired doctor who had provided Bram with a hideout on her farm in the Magaliesberg hills, Felicia Milindton, appeared in court, but despite prompting by the prosecution, remained vague. She described how a man calling himself Charles Thompson had asked if he could stay on the farm, saying he felt terribly upset about the death of his wife in a car accident and wanted to be away for a while. But she was unable to identify the man in court and claimed she had never heard of Bram Fischer.

Sholto Cross, called as a witness, described how he had gone for a picnic with Bram and Ilse to Hartbeespoortdam in October 1965. When asked why he had not reported Bram to the police, he replied: 'It was not morally right, even though it might have been legally right to do so.' When asked why he thought Bram had gone underground, he said: 'I would say that he felt it was a service to his country to do so.'

Lesley Schermbrucker, brought to court from prison where she was being held and interrogated under the 180-day law, refused to testify, saying she was prepared to face the consequences. 'I don't wish to be disrespectful and I don't want to go to jail, but it is a question of principle.' She was sentenced to 300 days' imprisonment. Her two children, aged 13 and 17, were now without both parents. Violet Weinberg also refused to testify, and was similarly punished. Both were subsequently sentenced to two years' imprisonment for helping Bram underground.

When Bram's trial opened on 23 March 1966 in the Palace of Justice in Pretoria, he sat alone in the 12-man dock in the central court which had been constructed especially for the Rivonia defendants. The charges he now faced were similar to the ones they had faced. In addition to being a member of the outlawed Communist Party, Bram was accused of sabotage and conspiring to cause 'a violent revolution' in South Africa.

The main burden of evidence against Bram came from a Communist Party defector, Bartholomew Hlapane, whom Joe Slovo had recruited in 1955. Appointed a full-time party organiser in 1961, he had joined the central committee in 1962 and had attended several key meetings before being detained in June 1963. Released after 172 days, he had been allowed to resume his place on the central committee in May 1964. Detained once more in September 1964, he had soon 'cracked'. His knowledge of Bram's underground activities was considerable. The other main witnesses for the prosecution were Piet Beyleveld and Gerard Ludi.

Then, with Ruth, Ilse and Paul listening ardently in the courtroom, Bram stood in the dock to give his testament as an Afrikaner revolutionary, explaining, in much the same way that Nelson Mandela had done during the Rivonia Trial, the reasons behind his defiance of the apartheid state:

> I am on trial for my political beliefs and for the conduct to which those beliefs drove me. Whatever labels may be attached to the 15 charges brought against me, they all arise from my having been a member of the Communist Party and from my activities as a member. I engaged upon those activities because I believed that, in the dangerous circumstances which have been created in South Africa, it was my duty to do so.
>
> When a man is on trial for his political beliefs and actions, two courses are open to him. He can either confess to his transgressions and plead for mercy or he can justify his beliefs and explain why he acted as he did. Were I to ask forgiveness today I would betray my cause. That course is not open to me. I believe that what I did was right. I must therefore explain to this court what my motives were: why I hold the beliefs that I do and why I was compelled to act in accordance with them.

He explained his reasons for pleading not guilty to the charges:

> I accept the general rule that for the protection of a society laws should be obeyed. But when laws themselves become immoral and require the citizen to take part in an organised system of oppression – if only by his silence or apathy – then I believe that a higher duty arises. This compels one to refuse to recognise such laws. The laws under which I am being prosecuted were enacted by a wholly unrepresentative body, a body in which three-quarters

of the people of this country have no voice whatever. These laws were enacted, not to prevent the spread of communism, but for the purpose of silencing the opposition of the large majority of our citizens to a government intent upon depriving them, solely on account of their colour, of the most elementary rights: of the right to freedom and happiness, the right to live together with their families wherever they may choose, to earn their livelihoods to the best of their abilities, to rear and educate their children in a civilised fashion, to take part in the administration of their country and obtain a fair share of the wealth they produce; in short, to live as human beings. My conscience does not permit me to afford these laws such recognition as even a plea of guilty would involve. Hence, though I shall be convicted by this court, I cannot plead guilty. I believe the future may well say that I acted correctly.

His first duty, he said, was to explain why South Africa's problems could only be solved without violence and civil war by the application of Marxism:

When I consider what it was that moved me to join the Communist Party, I have to cast my mind back for more than a quarter of a century to try and ascertain what precisely my motives at that time were.

Marxism is a system of philosophy which covers and seeks to explain the whole range of human activity, but looking back, I cannot say that it was Marxism as a social science that drew me originally to the Communist Party, just as little, presumably, as a doctor would say he was originally drawn to his own field of science by its scientifically demonstrable truths. These only became apparent later.

In my mind there remain two clear reasons for my approach to the Communist Party. The one is the glaring injustice which exists and has existed for a long time in South African society; the other, a gradual realisation, as I became more and more deeply involved with the Congress Movement of those years, that is, the movement for freedom and equal human rights for all, that it was always members of the Communist Party who seemed pre-pared, regardless of cost, to sacrifice most; to give of their best, to face the greatest dangers, in the struggle against poverty and discrimination.

Yet injustice by itself did not explain his conduct; it was there for all white South Africans to see. But the vast majority of whites remained unmoved and unaffected. He himself, during his youth, had shared the common white attitude towards Africans and understood it.

But, he explained, his experiences with the Joint Council in Bloemfontein had caused him to question white attitudes, and he recalled the incident when he felt revulsion at having to shake hands with a black man, lying awake at night wondering why, and realising that there was no rational basis for it.

The result of all this was that in that and in succeeding years when some of us ran literacy classes in the old Waaihoek location at Bloemfontein, I came to understand that colour prejudice was a wholly irrational phenomenon and that true human friendship could extend across the colour bar once the initial prejudice was overcome. And that I think was lesson no. 1 on my way to the Communist Party which has always refused to accept any colour bar and has always stood firm on the belief, itself 2 000 years old, of the eventual brotherhood of all men.

The other reason for his attraction to the Communist Party, he said, was the willingness of communists to make sacrifices. Regardless of the hatred that party members had to endure from the rest of the white community, they stood avowedly and unconditionally for polit-ical rights for non-whites.

These members, I found, were whites who could have taken full advantage of all the privileges open to them and their families because of their colour, who could have obtained lucrative employment and social position, but who, instead, were prepared for the sake of their consciences to perform the most menial and unpopular work at little or sometimes no remuneration. These

141

were a body of whites who were not prepared to flourish on the deprivation of others.

But apart from the example of the white members, it was always the communists of all races who were at all times prepared to give of their time and their energy and such means as they had, to help those in need and those most deeply affected by discrimination. It was members of the Communist Party who helped with night schools and feeding schemes, who assisted trade unions fighting desperately to preserve standards of living and who threw themselves into the work of national movements. It was African communists who constantly risked arrest or the loss of their jobs or even their homes in locations, in order to gain or retain some rights.

He spoke of 'a strong and ever-growing movement for freedom' in South Africa:

However complacent and indifferent white South Africa may be, this movement can never be stopped. In the end it must triumph. Above all, those of us who are Afrikaners and who have experienced our own successful struggle for full equality should know this.

The sole questions for the future were whether the change could be brought about peacefully and without bloodshed, and what the position of the white man was going to be in the period immediately following the establishment of democracy 'after the years of cruel discrimination and oppression and humiliation which he has imposed on the non-white peoples of this country'.

If today there is an appearance of calm, it is a false appearance induced entirely by this oppression. The police state does not create real calm or induce any genuine acceptance of a hated policy. All it can achieve is a short-term period of quiet and a long-term hatred.

The end result would be civil war.

Such a civil war can never be won by the whites of the country. They might win some initial rounds. In the long run, the balance of forces is against them ...

Win or lose, the consequences of civil war would be horrifying and permanent.

Bram spoke of his deep apprehension about the future of his own Afrikaner people, for it was Afrikaners who were blamed for all the evils and humiliations of apartheid:

All this bodes ill for the future. It has bred a deep-rooted hatred for Afrikaners, for our language, our political and racial outlook amongst all non-whites – yes, even amongst those who seek positions of authority by pretending to support apartheid. It is rapidly destroying amongst non-whites all belief in future co-operation with Afrikaners.

To remove this barrier will demand all the wisdom, leadership and influence of those Congress leaders now sentenced and imprisoned for their political beliefs. It demands also that Afrikaners themselves should protest openly and clearly against discrimination.

To ensure that at least one Afrikaner made this protest actively, he had undertaken the task himself.

It was to keep faith with all those dispossessed by apartheid that I broke my undertaking to the court, separated myself from my family, pretended I was someone else, and accepted the life of a fugitive. I owed it to the political prisoners, to the banished, to the silenced and those under house arrest, not to remain a spectator, but to act. I knew what they expected of me and I did it. I felt responsible, not to those who are indifferent to the sufferings of others but to those who are concerned.

At the end of his four-hour speech, Bram declared:

If one day it may help to establish a bridge across which white leaders and the real leaders of the non-whites can meet to settle

143

the destinies of all of us by negotiation and not by force of arms, I shall be able to bear with fortitude any sentence which this court may impose upon me. It will be a fortitude strengthened by this knowledge at least, that for 25 years I have taken no part, not even by passive acceptance, in that hideous system of discrimination which we have erected in this country and which has become a by-word in the civilised world today.

In prophetic words, in February 1881, one of the great Afrikaner leaders addressed the president and Volksraad of the Orange Free State. His words are inscribed on the base of the statue of President Kruger in the square in front of this court. After great agony and suffering after two wars they were eventually fulfilled without force or violence for my people. President Kruger's words were:

Met vertouwen leggen wy onze zaak open voor de geheele wereld. Het zy wy overwinnen, het zy wy sterven: de vryheid zal in Afrika ryzen als de zon uit de morewolken.

[With faith we lay our whole case bare to the world. Whether we win, whether we die, freedom shall rise over Africa as the sun out of the morning clouds.]

In the meaning which those words bear today they are as truly prophetic as they were in 1881. My motive in all I have done has been to prevent a repetition of that unnecessary pain and futile anguish which has already been suffered in our struggle for freedom.

On the night before he was sentenced, Bram wrote a letter to his children. 'My darlings. This is farewell – I think. We seem to have said it so often that I am growing somewhat sceptical about its ever happening. Goodness, we seem to have been through several lifetimes in the past two years, don't we?' He thanked them for the new birthday shirt they had sent him, which he said he would wear in court on the final day. 'All my love – Good luck.'

On 9 May 1966, at the age of 58, Bram was sentenced to life imprisonment. As the judge left the court, Bram turned round and smiled at Ilse and Paul sitting in the front row. Then he raised his hand and gave the salute of the African National Congress, before being led away.

CHAPTER 14

PRISONER 3331/66

From the Palace of Justice, Bram was taken back to Pretoria Local prison to begin life as a convicted prisoner. His cell was in a section of seven cells set aside for white political prisoners. The only other prisoner there at the time was Issy Heymann, who was serving a five-year sentence for membership of the Communist Party and a further year for refusing to give evidence against Bram. During Bram's trial, they had managed to have a few snatched conversations, standing on stools in their cells and speaking through wire-meshed grills adjoining the corridor. Issy had first attracted Bram's attention by whistling the opening line of *The Red Flag*, and Bram had responded by completing it, a routine they subsequently adopted. But this time, on his return from court, Bram sounded tired and depressed. Instead of standing on the stool, he remained sitting on the floor. 'He told me that he had received a life sentence. He said he was not going to appeal,' Issy recalled. 'There was a sob in his voice which he suppressed immediately and changed the subject before I could think of what to say to him.'

From then on, Bram was held in solitary confinement for weeks on end, having no contact with other prisoners. The warder in charge of the section, Head Warder du Preez, an Afrikaner, deliberately set out to make his life a misery, tormenting him at every available opportunity. He issued Bram with clothes that were far too large for him: a jacket with sleeves that hung below his hands, and trousers that he had to roll up. On the first day he arrived with hair clippers and snipped off most of Bram's hair, ignoring his protests. He once burst into Bram's cell, after seeing him reading after lunch, and threatened to confiscate his books. He was prone to outbursts of screaming, hurling abuse at will. He used every trick to break Bram, readily inflicting punishment for the slightest infringement of regulations. On his own, Bram possessed

145

no defence against such treatment. He remained courteous and polite, but slowly he was ground down.

A prisoner sent to the same section, Harold Strachan, remembered those months in 1966 as 'a time of vengeance'. A former Umkhonto instructor, imprisoned initially for his involvement in the manufacture of home-made bombs, Strachan had become an expert on the harsh regime imposed on prisoners. For a period of 11 months he had been held in solitary confinement – 'total silence for 11 months', as he remembered. After serving a three-year sentence, he had given a journalist a full account of prison conditions. In the ensuing uproar, the prison authorities were obliged to introduce reforms, but the price Strachan paid was to be sentenced to another 18 months for contravening the Prisons Act.

He arrived back in Pretoria Local in May 1966 at about the same time as Bram, but he knew nothing of Bram's whereabouts until an African warder told him one day that Bram was incarcerated in a nearby cell and wanted him to send him a note. The African warder said he would help provide a paper and pencil. Strachan feared a trap, but after two weeks succumbed to the temptation. 'Hello, Bram,' he wrote in Afrikaans. 'Keep courage and keep your head.' No sooner had he passed the note through the cell's mesh window to the African warder than the door opened and Du Preez entered. Strachan's punishment was six days without food.

The deadening routine of prison meanwhile stretched on day after day, week after week. Bram's cell contained no comfort. He had no bed but slept on the floor on two felt mats with a covering of two blankets. He was allowed a small table and a small wooden stool for furniture. His main possessions consisted of an enamel bowl for water, a tin mug, a washing bowl, and a toilet pot with a lid. For 23 hours a day he was confined to his cell. The only break from cell life was exercise periods in the prison yard.

During the first six months Bram was allowed to write and receive one letter limited to 500 words, and to meet one visitor for half an hour. His first visitor was Pat Davidson. They met in a bleak converted cell that served as a visiting room, sitting on either side of a table, separated by a perspex window with a warder standing behind each of them ready to terminate the visit if any forbidden topic was mentioned. Pat was nervous and tearful. 'He looked so small and lost,' she recalled. 'In his usual way, he tried to be cheerful. He didn't make any complaints. He asked about Ruth and Ilse and Paul. But it was not a good visit. I spent most of the time struggling to control myself.'

After three months of solitary existence, Bram was collected from his cell one day, and in the corridor encountered Strachan and Heymann. 'We didn't say anything,' recalled Strachan. 'There was just silent recognition of each other.'

The three prisoners were taken by Du Preez to the prison yard where there was an ablution block with urinals, two toilets and two showers surrounded by a low wall. They were told to wash the toilets and the urinals with soap and water, using rags and their bare hands. They were given brooms worn down to the wood to sweep the prison yard. For day after day this became their prison routine. Du Preez took particular delight in singling out Bram to clean the toilets, watching him work away with the rags on his hands and knees. 'It was a very purposeful insult,' recalled Strachan. 'He relished debasing Bram.' In the eyes of most Afrikaners, Bram was a traitor.

Bram said later that his life had been saved by the friendship and protection given to him by Heymann and Strachan during those grim months. 'Bram had no natural defence against arbitrary orders and vengeful actions,' recalled Strachan. 'He was used to kindness and courtesy.' Strachan taught Bram how to survive, and shielded him as best he could from the taunts and torments handed out by Du Preez and other warders. He became a close friend, providing Bram with not only protection but also intellectual stimulus. A former air force pilot, with a degree in fine art, he could recite Shakespeare and enjoyed reminiscing about journeys he had made in Europe. As part of his prison garb, Bram was issued with a greasy old felt hat. When he washed it in a bucket of boiling water, it turned into a shapeless faded rag. But Strachan sewed on to it a piece of green and red checked material which he had retrieved from the handstrap of a scrubbing brush. Bram became very attached to his headgear, and wore it for years.

Issy Heymann provided the humour. A short, warm-hearted man, he had a fund of Jewish jokes. 'Issy Heymann stood out for his generosity, his modesty, his endless good humour, and his giving of himself to assist others,' recalled Baruch Hirson, a prisoner who later joined the group. But Issy often fretted in private that it was his interrogation in detention that had led to Bram's capture. He made for Bram a waste-paper basket out of a large paper bag in which some stationery had arrived. When Du Preez saw it in Bram's call, he trampled on it and kicked it away. The regulations did not permit dustbins, said Du Preez.

In November 1966 a group of about 20 political prisoners being held in Pretoria Central were transferred to Bram's section in Pretoria Local, bringing together a sizeable prison community. Those who had known Bram beforehand were shocked to see how old and haggard he now appeared. 'We arrived in Pretoria Local in a boisterous mood to find Bram carrying his toilet pot and an enamel bowl of water balanced on it, silent and quiet,' recalled Denis Goldberg, one of the Rivonia trialists. 'He seemed fearful of antagonising warders. His strategy for survival had been to assume a quiet and modest demeanour.' One member of the group, Ivan Schermbrucker, took an immediate interest in Bram's welfare, and slowly he began to recover. Other old friends included Eli Weinberg and David Kitson.

The prisoners were a motley crowd. The largest group were members of the Communist Party. Others had belonged to the African Resistance Movement. A few were Maoists. Among their number were three lawyers, including Bram; four teachers; and four journalists including Marius Schoon and Hugh Lewin, who had been a close friend of Ruth in her schooldays.

Bram was given work sewing mailbags, sitting with four or five others in a circle of stools in the courtyard. During work periods and exercise breaks they argued about politics, spoke of their professional lives, and told and re-told of books read and films seen, of places visited and food eaten. There were numerous disputes and occasional friction. But mostly they continued to live in peace.

Bram's prison life steadily became more purposeful. He registered to study for a degree by correspondence course. He devoted considerable time to helping with other prisoners' problems, raising their complaints with the prison authorities. With his hair turning white, he became known as 'the Great White Father' or GWF. 'What endeared Bram to everyone in the prison yard was his lack of personal rancour, his even-handed treatment of everyone, and his compassion,' noted Baruch Hirson.

'Even in the worst of times,' remembered Hugh Lewin, 'it was always Bram who took on himself the problems of others, always Bram to whom they could turn for advice or encouragement or support, always Bram who knew first when anybody had a problem and who sought out that person and cheered them.'

Prison warders also sought Bram's advice on legal and family problems. He would spend hours patiently dealing with their tax returns or rent arrears or traffic offences. Senior officers invariably singled him out for attention. 'To the authorities, Bram in prison was a sort of prize exhibit, evoking a mixture of horror and respect and curiosity,' said Hugh Lewin. 'It was always Bram who was picked out for inspection and nodded at, always Bram who was greeted with "Hello, Bram" – as if the chance to greet him with familiarity somehow enhanced their position, somehow gave them added status. And Bram, usually with his battered brown hat in hand, would stand quietly, nod back and smile, always scrupulously polite and unbowed.'

In May 1967 Bram learned that he had been awarded the Lenin Peace Prize, but neglected to tell his fellow prisoners. When one of them found out from a visitor, they all clustered around him in the exercise yard to congratulate him. Bram was embarrassed, saying he saw it as a gesture of solidarity, not a personal award. He had accepted it, he told Ilse in a letter, 'only as a representative of people who are far braver than I and who have given far more'. In any case, he said, the award belonged as much to Molly as himself.

But his fellow prisoners were determined to mark the occasion, and prepared a hand-made greetings card which was slipped to him with his supper one afternoon at lock-up. Part of the tribute read:

This is your fight:
That other men might have the right to peace.
For this belief in man
we honour you.

A major improvement in prison life came in December 1968 when Bram's prisoner group was transferred to a new section within

Pretoria Local specially built for white political prisoners. For the first time in more than two-and-a-half years, Bram was able to sleep on a bed, with a mattress, pillow and sheets. His cell had a toilet, a basin with hot and cold running water, a fixed cupboard with a sliding table-leaf, and a bookshelf. From an outside window he could see into the yard below, and open and shut a section of the window at will. Meals were taken in the company of his fellow prisoners in a down-stairs dining room, seated at large, smart tables.

He was able to order his own books and watch the occasional film. Each evening music was played over loudspeakers in the corridor, chosen by prisoners themselves. Bram at one stage was appointed Chief Record Programmer. During exercise periods and at weekends he joined in sporting activity in the courtyard. Even at the age of 60 he retained his athletic skill, and was renowned for his devastating topspin in a prison version of tennis.

A section of the courtyard was set aside for a garden, and a number of prisoners, including Bram, were given the task of building one. For hours every working day, Bram toiled away in the garden, weeding, mowing, tending seedlings, and watering and training plants. 'The garden and the lawn became Bram's great concern,' recalled Issy Heymann. 'He used to go to the garden before breakfast to tend the flower beds.' Flowers grown by the prisoners were given to prison staff and to visitors. Working in the sun without a shirt, Bram took on a reddish-brown hue. He used to scatter crumbs of bread for the doves and other birds, calling them to come with a soft whistle.

In 1969 he was upgraded to a category 'B' prisoner, the second-highest level, which enabled him to write and receive two letters and enjoy a double visit every month. In letters to his children, he tried to involve himself in family life, advising on school education and careers, remembering Christmas and birthday presents, and com-menting on books he had read and flowers he was growing.

He was particularly pleased with Paul's progress. Despite his crip-pling ill-health, Paul had decided to study for an economics degree at Cape Town University. He spent a happy time in Cape Town, with Ilse looking after him, and managed to gain a second-degree pass in his honours course.

Despite the improvement in prison conditions, the prison authorities remained as vindictive as before. When Bram went to the prison commander, Captain Schnepel, to ask for extra minutes to a visit from his sister, Ada, who was dying of cancer, Schnapel brusquely refused. 'No – why should you have extra time? People are dying every day,' he said. It was Bram's last meeting with his sister. She died shortly afterwards.

Then, one evening in January 1971, Bram was abruptly summoned to meet an unexpected visitor. In the visitor's room, separated by a perspex partition, Bram found his brother, Gustav. He told Bram that Paul had died suddenly on 27 January after checking himself into Groote Schuur hospital. The prison authorities would not allow a contact visit, so the two brothers remained separated by the perspex screen, watched by prison warders. Then Bram was escorted back to his cell, and locked in for 14 hours to endure the long night alone. Captain Schnepel briefly came to see him to say he was sorry to hear the news.

Bram applied for permission to attend Paul's funeral. It was refused. When Ilse and Ruth came to see him, he was denied a contact visit. To fellow prisoners he remained steadfast, showing little sign of the anguish he felt. He never talked much about Paul, keeping his feelings to himself, bearing the burden alone, more concerned for others than for himself. In a letter to Ilse he wrote: 'I understand all the time what you are feeling – the deep depressions and the pain which is as if physical. For you it is worse than anyone since, for over five years, he was your constant companion and care. Yet, as your pain is greatest, your consolation too should be greatest. We all did what we could, given the initial tragedy of genes that went wrong, to make his life as full and happy as possible. But no one succeeded as much as you did ... For that Ruth and I owe you a debt we can never repay ...'

Later in the year, Ilse became engaged to Tim Wilson, a doctor from a distinguished South African family. They wanted to be married at a special ceremony in Pretoria Local which Bram would be able to attend. But prison regulations stipulated that Bram could receive only two visitors at a time, and the presence of a church minister meant that there would be three. So the prison authorities turned the request down.

151

Throughout his prison ordeal, Bram's commitment to the Communist Party and the Soviet Union never wavered. 'He held on to this great strategic vision of how we would defeat imperialism,' recalled Denis Goldberg. 'He saw socialism as a matter of life and death,' remarked John Laredo. Baruch Hirson, a Trotskyist, who worked in the garden with Bram, had numerous conversations with him. 'Talking to Bram about events in the USSR was an exercise in frustration. He steadfastly closed his ears to any criticism of what happened, past, present, or even future,' recalled Hirson. 'I disagreed with him on many issues and made clear my very profound hatred of Stalinism … but that never changed the respect and affection in which we held the man.'

One by one, as their prison sentences came to an end, Bram's companions departed, all of them touched for ever by the friendship they had shared with him. 'He had a strength that set him above all the needling and stings proffered by the authorities,' said Hirson. 'He towered over them as he towered over the political prisoners.' Marius Schoon recalled: 'Those blue eyes of Bram were like steel. He was principled about everything. Nothing was done outside those self-imposed principles. He had such commitment. Yet he was so tremendously warm.' Hugh Lewin left in 1977, knowing that Bram's friendship had been one of the most rewarding episodes of his life.

Numerous appeals were made for Bram's release. In April 1973, at the time of his sixty-fifth birthday, a group of distinguished white South Africans including Helen Suzman, the opposition member of parliament, Denis Hurley, archbishop of Durban, and Dr Christiaan Barnard, the heart-transplant pioneer, approached the government, but to no avail.

The following year his health began to deteriorate. For some time he had suffered from a number of minor ailments: arthritis in his left hip, which worsened during Pretoria's winter cold; eye trouble which had led to a cataract operation in 1969; and continuing ulcer problems. In May 1974 he was admitted to hospital for treatment to a perforated ulcer. In July his prostate was removed.

The prison authorities showed little concern for his health. The surgeon carrying out the prostatectomy suspected cancer, and ordered tests. Although the first tests were negative, he asked for more tests to be made, but the laboratory reports went missing and Bram received no further treatment. Worried by Bram's condition, Denis Goldberg began to keep a secret record of what occurred.

During September, the pain in Bram's hip became severe. He complained of it during a visit by Ilse and her husband, Dr Tim Wilson, a sign of how serious it was, since he rarely made any complaint. He asked the prison authorities for a crutch to help him walk, but was told at first that none was available. Only when his companions fashioned a crutch out of a broom did they agree to provide him with a proper one.

When Ilse and Tim visited Bram again a few weeks later, they found him propped up on crutches. Despite repeated requests he had still not been treated by a doctor. Tim wrote to the prison authorities, protesting that in his opinion as a doctor Bram was receiving grossly inadequate medical care. Only after this was Bram treated by a doctor. In October, after an X-ray examination, a specialist reported that the neck of his femur was very fragile, and warned of the danger of Bram falling.

On 6 November Bram slipped and fell while struggling into the shower on crutches. The following day, in intense pain, he asked to see a doctor, fearing a fracture, but no doctor arrived. He asked again the next day, but a medical orderly said it was impossible to get one. He was given analgesics. On 12 November a doctor decided that there was no fracture. But Bram remained in great pain and his mental state deteriorated. Nine days after the fall, an X-ray examination revealed a fracture at the neck of the femur. Thirteen days after the fall and four days after the fracture had been identified, Bram was finally admitted to hospital.

Bram stayed in hospital for two weeks, recovering from an operation to pin his femur, but despite his serious condition he was returned to prison on 4 December. His prison colleagues found him alone in a wheelchair in the dining room, confused and unable to speak. By midafternoon he was running a high temperature and was unable to help himself. For the next two days and nights, as he lay delirious with fever, Denis Goldberg nursed him in his cell, feeding him, washing him, and carrying him to the toilet, while the prison authorities and the doctors ignored his plight. He was so light, said Goldberg, that he could carry him anywhere. 'It was a joy to do what was needed; terribly sad that it was needed,' recalled Goldberg. 'That's when I did my crying – in December, when I realised he had cancer and that he'd soon be gone.'

On 6 December Bram was readmitted to hospital. The cancer which had been suspected six months before was now ravaging his body. It was obvious he had little time to live. He soon fell into a semi-coma. But treated with radiotherapy, he recovered sufficiently to be able to get up and walk a few steps with the help of a metal frame. Ruth brought her daughter, Gretel, to see him, giving him a special joy in his last months.

Yet still the government would not relent, ignoring desperate appeals from around the world for his release. The minister of justice, Jimmy Kruger, claimed in parliament that Bram had not changed his communist beliefs and represented a security risk. If released, he would inevitably go to live with his family in Johannesburg, the city with 'the greatest percentage of subversives'.

Only in March, with Bram's strength steadily failing, did the government agree to let him spend his last days with his family. Even then, officials remained vindictive to the end. Instead of releasing him to his daughters, they had him transferred to his brother Paul's house in Bloemfontein, which they designated a prison, subject to prison regulations. Special permission had to be sought by friends wishing to visit him.

Bram's last weeks were spent in Bloemfontein, surrounded by his family, Ruth and Ilse and Gretel, sitting on the veranda, sipping tea and reading magazines. When he again needed radiotherapy, the local prison commander, Colonel Scheffer, collected him, carefully lifting him into his own car. On the way back to his brother's house one day, Bram asked to be driven past the prison where at the age of six he had visited rebel prisoners.

Soon after his sixty-fifth birthday he lapsed into unconsciousness and died two weeks later, on 8 May 1975.

Even then, the prison authorities were not finished with him. Within an hour of being notified of his death, prison officers arrived at Paul Fischer's house with a list of conditions concerning the funeral arrangements. They stipulated that the family could have the body for the funeral, provided that this was held in Bloemfontein within a week and that, in the event of cremation, his ashes must be returned to the Department of Prisons.

At a simple ceremony in Bloemfontein, the lawyer Arthur Chaskalson read out a speech written in London by Bram's former prison colleague, Hugh Lewin:

Do not weep for Bram. He would not have you weep on his behalf. And do not weep for the recent long years in jail. That, especially, he would not like. For though they were long, painful years away from his family and his friends outside, for Bram inside they were not lost years. They meant for Bram, in a very real sense, a rounding and a completion.

However full the man who first went to jail – however distinguished the lawyer, however fine the father, husband, friend, adviser – however full the man before, jail encompassed the fullness and enlarged it.

In the beginning, prison stripped Bram bare – in a process which, for him, was even more severe and complete than it is for most. It stripped him of the protection of a respected position and of privilege and esteem, and denied him what had always been so dear to him, the comfort of family and friends and familiar surroundings.

But, in so denuding him, prison in fact gave Bram something new. In seeking to stifle him, it gave him new vigour. It sought to hide him and succeeded only in revealing the simple, essential greatness of the man.

The Afrikaner writer, André Brink, added his own eulogy. Far from alienating himself from his Afrikaner people, he said, Bram had 'enlarged and deepened' the concept of Afrikanerdom. 'If Afrikanerdom is to survive, it may well be as a result of the broadening and liberating influence of men like Bram Fischer.' Fischer's true cause went beyond the confines of a political system. He believed in liberty, justice, compassion, trust, equality of mercy and, above all, human dignity. 'It is my firm belief that in his pursuit of these ideals, history will not only absolve him but vindicate him.'

EPILOGUE

On 9 June 1995, a year after South Africans had participated in their first democratic elections, President Nelson Mandela arrived at the Market Theatre in Johannesburg to pay tribute to Bram Fischer and to inaugurate a lecture series commemorating his name.

'Bram Fischer,' said Mandela, 'was a great advocate and a great patriot.' He had followed the most difficult course any person could choose to follow. 'He challenged his own people because he felt that what they were doing was morally wrong.' If he had chosen to follow the path of Afrikaner nationalism, he could have become prime minister or chief justice. 'He chose instead the long and hard road to freedom not only for himself but for all of us. He chose the road that had to pass through jail. He travelled it with courage and dignity. He served as an example to many who followed him.'

An equally moving tribute, one that Bram would have particularly enjoyed, came from his colleagues in the legal profession. In October 1997 the Johannesburg Bar Council apologised for the grave injustice done by striking him from the roll of advocates. A special memorandum drawn up by the General Council of the Bar affirmed Bram 'a most honourable and trustworthy member of the Bar' who had 'at all times observed the highest ethical standards of legal practice' and who had been 'in every respect a worthy and distinguished member of the legal profession'.

The memorandum quoted from an account of Bram's case by the lawyer Geoff Budlender:

The story of Bram Fischer dramatises and illuminates the difficult question of what the duty of conscientious lawyers is, when the government (and particularly a non-representative government) represses its citizens. Many options present themselves. Does one

156

simply go about one's business, hoping that this unpleasantness will go away? Should one work within the (immoral) system as a lawyer, trying to mitigate the evils of the system and to assist those who are its victims? Or should one distance oneself completely, and attempt actively to undermine and subvert the system?

Bram Fischer's life demonstrates that the first option was never acceptable to him. He appears to have attempted to follow the second option for a long time. And then he ultimately chose the third option – resistance and rebellion – because in his words:

> I can no longer serve justice in the way I have attempted to do during the past 30 years. I can only do it in the way I have now chosen.

These are difficult questions, which will and should trouble all lawyers in all places. Honourable people have to attempt to make honourable choices. The story of Bram Fischer shows that it is the third option – Fischer's option – which is the most difficult, and which requires the greatest idealism and the greatest self-sacrifice.

Thus was Bram Fischer's life remembered by a new South African generation.

SELECT BIBLIOGRAPHY

Benson, Mary. *A Far Cry, The Making of a South African*. Randburg: Ravan Press, 1996.

Bernstein, Hilda. *The World That Was Ours*. London: Heinemann, 1967.

Bernstein, Hilda. *Death is Part of the Process*. London: Grafton, 1986.

Bernstein, Rusty *Memory Against Forgetting: Memoirs from a Life in South African Politics, 1938-1964*. Johannesburg: Penguin, 1999.

Brokensha, Miles and Knowles, Robert. *The Fourth of July Raids*. Cape Town: Simondium, 1965.

Clingman, Stephen. *Bram Fischer: Afrikaner Revolutionary*. Cape Town: David Philip, 1998.

De Villiers, HHW. *Rivonia: Operation Mayibuye*. Johannesburg: Afrikaanse Pers, 1964.

First, Ruth. *One Hundred and Seventeen Days*. Harmondsworth: Penguin, 1965.

Frankel, Glenn. *Rivonia's Children*. London: Weidenfeld and Nicolson, 1999.

Gordimer, Nadine. *Burger's Daughter*. Harmondsworth: Penguin, 1980.

Hirson, Baruch. *Revolutions in My Life*. Johannesburg: Witwatersrand University Press, 1995.

Joffe, Joel. *The Rivonia Story*. Bellville: Mayibuye Books, 1995.

Joseph, Helen. *If This be Treason*. London: Deutsch, 1963.

Joseph, Helen. *Tomorrow's Sun*. London: Hutchinson, 1966.

Joseph, Helen. *Side by Side: The Autobiography of Helen Joseph*. London: Zed Books, 1986.

Kasrils, Ronnie. *Armed and Dangerous: My Undercover Struggle Against Apartheid*. Oxford: Heinemann, 1993.

Lazerson, Joshua N. *Against the Tide: Whites in the Struggle Against Apartheid*. Bellville: Mayibuye Books, 1994.

Lewin, Hugh. *Bandiet: Seven Years in a South African Prison*. London: Barrie and Jenkins, 1974.

Ludi, Gerard. *Operation Q-018*. Cape Town: Nasionale Boekhandel, 1969.

Ludi, Gerard and Grobbelaar, Blaar. *The Amazing Mr Fischer*. Cape Town: Nasionale Boekhandel, 1966.

Mandela, Nelson *Long Walk to Freedom*. London: Little, Brown & Co., 1994

Meredith, Martin. *Nelson Mandela*. London: Penguin, 1997.

Middleton, Jean. *Convictions: A Woman Political Prisoner Remembers*. Randburg: Ravan Press, 1999.

Mitchison, Naomi. *A Life for Africa: The Story of Bram Fischer*. London: Merlin Press, 1973.

Sampson, Anthony. *Mandela*. London: HarperCollins, 1999.

Slovo, Gillian. *Every Secret Thing*. London: Little, Brown & Co., 1997.

Slovo, Joe. *Slovo: The Unfinished Autobiography*. Randburg: Ravan Press, 1995.

Strydom, Lauritz. *Rivonia Unmasked!* Johannesburg: Voortrekkerpers, 1965.

Vermaak, Chris. *Bram Fischer: The Man with Two Faces*. Johannesburg, APB, 1966.

Wolpe, AnnMarie. *The Long Way Home*. Cape Town: David Philip, 1994.

INDEX

Schnepel, Captain 151
Schoon, Marius 57, 148, 152
Schoop, Diane 116
Schoop, Raymond 116, 123, 124, 126, 127, 132
Sepel, Mini 55, 116, 126, 127, 131, 135, 136
Sepel, Ralph 55, 73, 116, 126, 127, 131, 134, 135, 136
Sharpeville 48, 49, 55, 56
Simon, Barney 73
Simons, Jack 106, 130
Simons, Ray 106, 130
Sisulu, Walter 35, 36, 39, 40, 41, 48, 69, 78, 82, 93, 99, 101, 102, 106
Slovo, Gillian 62, 87
Slovo, Joe 42, 46, 47, 48, 50, 52, 58, 62, 63, 68, 69, 76, 77, 84, 87, 93, 112, 138
Smith, Nakie 7
Smuts, General Jan 16, 17, 28, 33
Sophiatown 56, 57
South African Communist Party see Communist Party, South African
South African Peace Council 41, 43
South African Society for Peace and Friendship with the Soviet Union 41, 43
Soviet Union (Russia) 20, 21, 28, 29, 36, 44, 68, 70, 152
Special Branch 42, 43, 46, 48, 50, 55, 56, 60, 61, 72, 91
Spitskop 8
St John's College 37
Stalin, Joseph 36, 58
Stalin's Five Year Plan see Five Year Plan
Stalingrad 20
Steyn, Colin 29
Steyn, Ouma 13, 15, 25, 122
Steyn, President Martinus 5, 6, 7
Strachan, Harold 146, 147
Suppression of Communism Act 34, 40, 41, 43, 66, 69, 84, 110
Suzman, Helen 152

Swanepoel, Theunis 94
Swart, Charles ('Oom Blackie') 36, 37
Swaziland 74
Tambo, Oliver 39, 50
The Road to South African Freedom 67
Thompson, Charles 138
Time for Reassessment 89
Transvaal Peace Council 41
Transvaler, Die 71
Travallyn 68, 69, 92
Trollope, Anthony 6
Turok, Ben 42, 44, 55, 76
Turok, Mary 42
Umkhonto we Sizwe 63, 64, 65, 68, 69, 71, 72, 74, 75, 76, 82, 93, 97, 98, 99, 100, 107, 115, 137, 146
Umtentweni 24
University of the Witwatersrand 30
Uys, Stanley 87
Van den Bergh, Hendrik 66
Veglio, Gabriella see Getcliffe, Ann
Verwoerd, Hendrik 65
Vienna 21, 41
Vorster, John 65, 66, 69, 125
Waaihoek location 14, 16
Weinberg, Eli 42, 50, 76, 105, 110, 113, 114, 130, 148
Weinberg, Mark 53
Weinberg, Violet 42, 43, 50, 57, 116, 127, 128, 131, 133, 134, 138
Wilson, Tim 151, 153
Windhoek 24, 25
Witwatersrand (Wits) University see University of the Witwatersrand
Wolpe, AnnMarie 66, 67, 71, 72, 73
Wolpe, Harold 61, 66, 67, 71, 72, 73, 74, 75, 82, 84, 94, 111
World Peace Council 41
Xuma, Alfred 30
Youth League see African National Congress Youth League
Yutar, Percy 81, 84, 87, 92, 94, 98, 100, 102